MASTERS
of the
ZHANG ZHUNG NYENGYUD:
Pith Instructions from the
Experiential Transmission of Bönpo Dzogchen

Teachings by Yongdzin Lopön Tenzin Namdak

Transcribed and edited by
Carol Ermakova and Dmitry Ermakov

HERITAGE

HERITAGE PUBLISHERS
19-A, Ansari Road, Daryaganj,
New Delhi - 110 002

HERITAGE PUBLISHERS

19-A, Ansari Road, Daryaganj,
New Delhi - 110 002
Tel.: 23266258, 23264444
Fax.: 23263050
E-mail: heritage@nda.vsnl.net.in

ISBN: 978-81-7026-268-8

Printed in India at
Thomson Press (India) Ltd.

Contents

Dedicated to the long life of Yongdzin Tenzin Namdak Rinpoche.
May this precious lineage remain unbroken!

PREFACE

When requested to write a Preface for this book, Yongdzin Rinpoche suggested instead that he could translate a passage from a text. This is the excerpt he kindly chose.

"When teaching *Zhang Zhung Nyengyud* Dzogchen one must follow certain rules, and there are four main ones.

First of all, there is the transmission which develops wisdom and one is not allowed to add any other quotations to this. The reason is that this transmission of wisdom is complete and has no need of any additional quotations taken from any other sources. Everything has already been clearly explained and commented on by qualified Masters. The Natural State is pure, clear and prefect. For example, if you take a lantern into a dark room it can make the whole room light; you don't need any additional source of light.

The second rule is connected with the lineage or transmission of the meaning which purifies mistakes and delusions. Misunderstandings are purified by valid cognition, and so one must not keep one's own footnotes or add one's own comments. The reason for this is that anyone who studies or follows these teachings must learn properly and not be dependent on what is said or written. This single lineage of knowledge passes strictly from Master to Master; each Master makes it clear and shows the real meaning, so there is no need to rely on additional notes or commentaries. It is like the following example: if someone is explaining what a flower is, the person listening will not be able to fully comprehend its colour or shape. If, however, the listener is directly shown the actual flower then not so many explanations are needed: they can see it for themselves.

The third rule is that the transmission of the pith instructions comes only through experience, through practice. There is no need to add human words or comments to this. For example, if you use

Tibetan words to comment on the Zhang Zhung language then it cannot be so useful; the Tibetan words cannot clearly describe the Zhang Zhung ones. The reason for this rule is that the teachings themselves are like solid gold which cannot be refined. So if a normal person tries to comment on them using normal words, they cannot.

The fourth rule is that someone who has received transmission of these teachings, who has practised them, trusts them and has obtained the result or final goal, may not add anything or be influenced by sectarian thoughts or comments. The reason for this relates to the way you should trust or believe. The text, the Master's explanation and what he has introduced to the student, as well as the follower's own experience, should all agree. When these three come together there is no need to add any comments. This trust is trust in one's own valid cognition and when one has obtained this valid cognition there is no partiality, just as one cannot divide space saying: this is my space, that is his space.

Furthermore, the Master who teaches Dzogchen must be qualified to do so, and whoever listens to the teachings must also have certain qualities.

As regards the qualities a true Master should possess, he must firstly have a verifiable lineage of transmission through which he received the teachings. Secondly, one should observe how he teaches his student. We can check how the Master received the teachings and lineage, and it is essential that he received teachings on the Nature of the Base without any additions or mistakes, and that his knowledge of this Natural State is equally free from additions or errors. There are two points regarding how he must have received the teachings; one is extremely important, the other less so: Firstly he should have received the *lung*, or reading transmission, but that is less important. What is most important is that along with this transmission he must have practised without mistakes so that he becomes familiar with this State and is able to remain stable in it. That is very important.

There are three points relating to how a Master receives his special lineage:
First of all he must receive the transmission from the authentic source;
Secondly he must receive the transmission and introduction to the pith instructions;
And thirdly, having received these, he must practise what he has received until a sign comes.

However, if the Master has broken any of these – for example, if he has not received the lineage in the proper way – then whatever his students practise and whatever he practises himself will not be of much use. It will be like churning water: butter will never be obtained.

Similarly, if the Master has not practised with the proper motivation or has not received the sign, then his teachings and words will just be like blowing up a balloon.

Thus the source and the lineage are both extremely important. It is very, very important to keep the history of the lineage."

[Taken from *sTod thun gyi 'grel ba bzhugs so*]

"Dzogchen sometimes seems easy but it is hard, very hard. We are always saying that we need to purify ourselves in many ways, but here we say there is only the Natural State, so although it sometimes looks easy, in fact the Natural State is very difficult to realize."

Yongdzin Lopön Tenzin Namdak Rinpoche
31st July, 2009
Tenth day of the sixth month of the Earth Elephant Year
Shenten Dargye Ling, Blou, France

FOREWORD

"The Yungdrung Bön tradition was founded by Tonpa Shenrab who taught three main teachings: the Path of Renunciation, the Path of Transformation and the Path of Liberation. From these three major groups, the most important or essential is the Dzogchen teachings of the great oral tradition of Zhang Zhung, the *Zhang Zhung Nyengyud*. This Teaching has come down from the Buddha to the present day in an unbroken lineage through a line of highly realized Masters who transmitted the instructions from one to another, from mouth to ear. Thus they have passed in an unbroken single lineage from Kuntu Zangpo up to my own root lama, the great and kind Yongdzin Lopön Tenzin Namdak Rinpoche.

The key instructions contained in the *Zhang Zhung Nyengyud* are extremely important as by following them it takes only a single lifetime to achieve Buddhahood; through practising these precious teachings, many great practitioners, including Shardza Tashi Gyaltsen and his students as well as the Masters presented in this volume, achieved Rainbow Body in one lifetime.

In the Yungdrung Bön tradition, Dzogchen is taught according to the capacity of the students – high, middling or lower. Most Dzogchen cycles include three main parts: firstly the Ngöndro – preparing and ripening the mind by means of all the diverse aspects of the preliminary practices; secondly, there are the teachings by which we can realize the true Nature of Mind and experience self-arising awareness for ourselves; and thirdly there are the teachings on integration and Thögal practices such as dark retreat, sky gazing and so on. Whoever follows these teachings must try their best to receive authentic instructions, especially the experiential teachings of a truly qualified Master, and to gain their own experience. Then understanding will follow.

Masters of the Zhang Zhung Nyengyud gives us the pith instructions of the Masters belonging to *Nyamgyud*, the experiential transmission, as taught by the current holder of this single lineage tradition, Yongdzin Lopön Tenzin Namdak Rinpoche. His disciples, Carol and Dmitry Ermakovi, have transcribed and edited these oral instructions. I am very happy that this book is coming out. Many, many thanks for all the hard work which has gone into it."

Geshe Gelek Jinpa
4th November 2009
17th day of the ninth month of the Earth Elephant Year
Oxford, Great Britain

ACKNOWLEDGEMENTS

This book has been made possible by the great kindness of Yongdzin Tenzin Namdak Rinpoche who not only taught many sections of the *Zhang Zhung Nyengyud* to his Western students but also encouraged us to make these pith instructions available to the wider public. We are deeply grateful to him for clarifying many points as we worked on preparing this text for publication, and also for his invaluable input in reconstructing the branches of the lineage.

We would also like to express our gratitude to Khenpo Tenpa Yungdrung and Geshe Namdak Nyima for their precious help in verifying the sequence of lineage Masters.

Thanks go to Geshe Gelek Jinpa for his support and advice, as well as for his readiness to write a Foreword, and to the Rev. Alan Stears and his wife, Pearl, whose generous support has been a great help throughout this project.

Graham Hill, Molly Thoron-Duran and Richard Williamson kindly proof-read this manuscript, and we are grateful for their input.

INTRODUCTION

In this book we present an edited transcript of teachings on *rDzogs pa chen po zhang zhung snyan rgyud kyi nyams rgyud skya ru bzhugs pa legs so*, known as *Chyaru*[1] for short, given by the current Lineage Holder, Yongdzin Lopön Tenzin Namdak Rinpoche, in Cergy near Paris in 1999. Over the centuries, the testaments of the Masters of the Single Lineage[2] of the *Zhang Zhung Nyengyud* have been collected into three versions: short, medium and long. This text belongs to the long version.[3]

   Despite the great significance of this text – both historically as it is an unbroken line of transmission and for practitioners as it contains the essential teachings of great Masters – very little has been published on it in English. The first publication was *The Little Luminous Boy* by Samten G. Karmay which came out in 1998.[4] A wonderful book which sheds light on the lives of the *Zhang Zhung Nyengyud* Masters and provides us with some images, it also partially explores the Experiential Transmission lineage within the context of a text summarizing the life-stories of the Masters.[5] More recently, John Myrdhin Reynolds[6] released his translations of some *Zhang Zhung Nyengyud* texts in *The Oral Tradition from Zhang-Zhung*, a valuable contribution to the materials on the *Zhang Zhung Nyengyud* and

---

[1] Tib. skya ru.
[2] Tib. gcig brgyud.
[3] The three collections are: Tib. Zhang zhung snyan rgyud kyi bla ma'i nyams rgyud bsdus pa thor bu; Zhang zhung snyan rgyud kyi bla ma'i nyams rgyud 'bring po sor bzhag; Zhang zhung snyan rgyud kyi bla ma'i nyams rgyud rgyas pa skya smug gnyis.
[4] Karmay, Samten G. *The Little Luminous Boy* (Bangkok: White Orchid Press, 1998).
[5] Tib. brGyud pa'i bla ma'i nam thar.
[6] Reynolds, John Myrdhin. *The Oral Tradition of Zhang-Zhung: An Introduction to the Bonpo Dzogchen Teachings of the Oral Tradition from Zhang-Zhung known as the Zhang-zhung snyan-rgyud* (Kathmandu: Vajra Publications, 2005).

Yungdrung Bön available to the Western public.

This book, *Masters of the Zhang Zhung Nyengyud,* is different in that for the first time, Yongdzin Rinpoche's teachings on the *Zhang Zhung Nyengyud* are being made publically available. While this oral commentary remains faithful to the original text, it reaches beyond the horizon of scholarly translations because Yongdzin Rinpoche himself is the current holder of this Single Lineage, so his interpretation carries the live current of this exceedingly ancient Bönpo Dzogchen[7] transmission; Rinpoche's clarifications, based on his own experience, profoundly enhance our understanding of the deep meaning contained in these Masters' last words.

Also included are colour reproductions of the *tsakali* initiation cards generously provided by Yongdzin Rinpoche so that each Master's testament can be matched to his image. Although traditionally a Master's final words are associated with the image of his successor, here the image of each Master is printed alongside his own teachings. The teachings of the Experiential Transmission are transmitted as an initiation with the students visualizing each Master and practising Lamai Naljyor or Guru Yoga while listening to his final advice.

Since this book you hold in your hand contains the direct words of the current lineage holder, Yongdzin Lopön Tenzin Namdak Rinpoche, it carries not only words and stories but also blessings, and as such it can become a key to unlock the doors of one's mind, a guide on the path to the realization of one's own Nature of Mind.

Dzogchen from Zhang Zhung

Since the Masters whose final teachings or testaments are contained in this book belong to the Bönpo Dzogchen lineage of Zhang Zhung, it is important to say a couple of words about this ancient country. Zhang Zhung was an empire or tribal confederation which controlled most of the Tibet-Qinghai Plateau, exerting cultural, religious and political influence on cultures of the regions far beyond its fluctuating borders – into the Himalayas in the South; into Gilgit and Kashmir in the West; into the Tarim Basin of Mongolia and even Southern Siberia in the North; and into China in the East.[8] According to traditional Bönpo

---

[7] Tib. rdzogs chen.

[8] For more on possible routes along which Bönpo culture may have spread in and around Zhang Zhung see Dmitry Ermakov, *Bø and Bön: Ancient Shamanic Traditions of Siberia and Tibet in their relation to the Teachings of a Central Asian Buddha,* (Kathmandu: Vajra Publications, 2008), pp. 706-745.

sources, Yungdrung Bön was brought to Zhang Zhung from Tagzig by Tonpa Shenrab Miwo[9] himself at the time of the reign of the first Zhang Zhung king Triwer Lhaje Gulang Sergyi Gyaruchen,[10] The Holder of the Golden Khyung[11] Horned Crown. The practitioners of the belief system preceding Yungdrung Bön, Prehistoric Domai Bön,[12] who worshipped various classes of gods and spirits, were gradually converted and Yungdrung Bön took root. With time, all levels of Dö, Gyud[13] and Dzogchen belonging to Yungdrung Bön or Bön Nyingma,[14] known in Zhang Zhung by its original name Drungmu Gyer,[15] were transmitted and practised in Zhang Zhung, spreading out from there in all directions. While Dö and Gyer were written down as texts, the Dzogchen tradition remained entirely oral in Zhang Zhung until it was written down by Nangzher Lödpo in the eighth century AD. Yungdrung Bön came to the fledgling Tibetan state from Zhang Zhung at its very inception, at the time of the first Tibetan king Nyatri Tsenpo, and became the foundation upon which the Tibetan Empire was built. It penetrated all aspects of Tibetan religious and secular life deeply, but in the eighth century Yungdrung Bön suffered severe damage due to political and religious repressions instigated by Trisong Deutsen and a party of overzealous converts to Indian Buddhism. However, the great saint and Tantric adept Guru Padmasambhava, who brought Tantric Buddhism to Tibet, seems not to have been involved in this persecution, as some sectarian Buddhist scholars would have us believe. Instead, he actively participated in preserving some of Yungdrung Bön's teachings and adapted many Bönpo methods to his own tradition, thus creating the unique Tibetan Buddhism.

It was at this time that the third Drenpa Namkha,[16] a Bönpo Drubthob[17] (Mahasiddha), and the Buddhist translator Vairotsana of Pagor,[18] created their own system of practice known as Bön Sarma[19]

---

[9] Tib. sTon pa gShen rab Mi bo.
[10] Tib. Khri wer La rje Gu lang gSer gyi Bya ru can.
[11] Tib. khyung is an indigenous Zhang Zhung and Tibetan mythical horned eagle often translated as *garuda*.
[12] Tib. gdod ma'i bon.
[13] Tib. mdo, rgyud – original Bönpo terms corresponding to the Sanskrit terms Sutra and Tantra.
[14] Tib. bon rnying ma.
[15] Tib. drung mu gyer.
[16] There were three sages by the same name, successive reincarnations of the same Master who first appeared on a blue lotus in Zhang Zhung long ago. For more information see Ermakov, *Bo and Bön*, pp.144-148.
[17] Tib. grub thob.
[18] Tib. sPa gor Bai ro tsa na.

or New Bön. This syncretic system also combined elements of Bön and Indian Buddhism but while in Padmasambhava's system the doctrinal foundation was firmly based on the Sanskrit Buddhist texts of Indian Buddhism, Bön Sarma's doctrinal foundations are rooted in the Bönpo *Katen*[20] or 'Original Words' of Tonpa Shenrab Miwo. This system of practice is still very much alive today and is spread particularly widely in Kham, Eastern Tibet.[21] Even when the Sarma Schools of Tibetan Buddhism came into existence centuries later, they became so profoundly influenced by Yungdrung Bön that after completing his study of Tibetan Buddhist and Bönpo doctrines, the eighteenth century Gelugpa scholar Thuvan Chökyi Nyima[22] commented:

'Bön is so mingled with Buddhism and Buddhism with Bön that my analytic eye fails to see the difference between them.'[23]

We can say, then, that the threads of the ancient Bön of Zhang Zhung run not only within Tibetan culture in general but also within each School of Tibetan Buddhism. And so the Bönpo culture of Zhang Zhung remains as a foundation of Tibetan culture and society, continuing to serve Tibetan people in their spiritual and secular lives today regardless of whether they are Bönpo or Buddhist.

Despite the damage Yungdrung Bön suffered in the eighth century and despite the external influence from incoming Indian Buddhism, the heart of the tradition was preserved intact so that the teachings and practice methods taught by Tonpa Shenrab are still being practised and passed on today in their original form. While many Yungdrung Bön scriptures were concealed in the eighth century to be discovered later, as Nyingma *termas*[24] were, some texts, like the *Zhang Zhung Nyengyud*, have never been concealed but have been taught and practised continuously without interruption.

The *Zhang Zhung Nyengyud* was not the only Dzogchen cycle spread in Zhang Zhung. However, the teachings contained in the two other major Dzogchen cycles – *bsGrags pa skor gsum*, *The Three Cycles of Propagation*, and *Sems smad sde dgu*, *The Nine Cycles of*

---

[19] Tib. bon gsar ma.

[20] Tib. bka' rten.

[21] For a detailed presentation on Bönpo history and different types of Bön see Ibid. pp. 1-58, 129-162.

[22] Tib. Thu'u bkvan Chos kyi nyi ma.

[23] Karmay, Samten G. *The Arrow and the Spindle: Studies in History, Myths, Rituals and Beliefs in Tibet* (Kathmandu: Mandala Book Point, 1998), p. 533.

[24] Tib. gter ma.

the Lesser Mind Series – had to be hidden as *terma* during the persecution of the eighth century. This makes the *Zhang Zhung Nyengyud* unique among all other Dzogchen cycles, Bönpo or Buddhist. Firstly, since it came into this dimension at the time of Tonpa Shenrab himself it is the most ancient lineage of Dzogchen on earth, and secondly, since it has never been concealed, it has enjoyed an uninterrupted transmission from Kuntu Zangpo right down to us. As such it contains pure, unaltered Dzogchen teachings and methods with nothing added or taken away, and enhanced with the enormous power of spiritual blessings.

The preservation, purity and continuity of the meaning and blessings of this cycle are safeguarded by strict rules governing its transmission. Whoever transmits the *Four Cycles of Precepts* must have four special qualifications which are explained in the Outer Cycle, in the text *lTaba spyi gcod kyi mnyam bzhag sgom pa'i lag len*:

[A *Zhang Zhung Nyengyud* Master must:]
    '1. have received transmission purely in an unbroken lineage;
    2. know the meaning of the text without mixing it with others such as Sutra, Tantra or other Dzogchen teachings. It should be kept pure;
    3. not merely be able to repeat the text but also must have practised and gained experience;
    4. not be influenced by other lineages or texts, but keep this lineage purely.
    It is limited to such Masters.'[25]

Because of these conditions the teachings of the *Zhang Zhung Nyengyud* have come down to us unadulterated and pure, exactly as Sangwa Düpa[26] transmitted them to Lhabön Yongsu Dagpa.

The Path of Dzogchen

The wisdom teachings presented in this book are experiential instructions given by realized Masters of Dzogchen who practised this path and obtained its highest fruit – the realization of the Rainbow Body of Light, or Jalu.[27] For those who realize Rainbow Body, death

---

[25] Tenzin Namdak, Trnscr. & ed. Carol Ermakova and Dmitry Ermakov, *Nyam-zhag Gom-pa'i Lag-len: Teachings by Lopön Tenzin Namdak Rinpoche given at the Shamabhala Centre, Paris, April 1997*, (Shenten Dargye Ling, 2005), p.1.

[26] Tib. gSang ba 'Dus pa

[27] Tib. 'ja' lus. There are three main types of Rainbow Body. The highest level is called Tib. 'ja' lus 'pho ba chen po – the Rainbow Body of the Great Transfer. At this

does not manifest in the usual manner; instead, the physical body visibly dissolves into the essence of the elements without leaving any remains behind. This realization is no trick or magic of some sort but is the natural outcome of Dzogchen practice when it is brought to its full completion. A Dzogchen practitioner at this stage achieves complete purification of karma as his or her impure vision dissolves back into its source, the Nature of Mind.[28] The Three Bodies of Sanggye - Bönku, Dzogku and Trülku - are realized simultaneously.[29]

In Yungdrung Bön, Bön Sarma and the Nyingma[30] School of Tibetan Buddhism, the teachings and practice of Dzogchen are considered the ultimate, supreme way among all other ways. The vehicles of Sutra and Tantra are viewed as provisional from the Dzogchen perspective as they do not deal directly with the Source of All,[31] the Nature of Mind, but always rely on consciousness as the means to obtain purification. The vehicle of Sutra uses the methods of renunciation; the vehicle of Tantra uses the methods of transformation, and both employ mental effort in order to progress along the path towards liberation. Dzogchen is unique among all other

level a practitioner becomes a complete Buddha in his or her very body. Unnoticed by others, the physical body of such a practitioner is transformed into the essence of the five elements, the five pure lights (Tib. 'od lnga); such a person does not manifest any signs of death. This kind of being can disappear and reappear on this mundane plane at any point in time or space in response to the needs of those seeking the path of realization. The early Masters of the *Zhang Zhung Nyengyud*, as well as yogis from other lineages of Bönpo Dzogchen, such as Tsewang Rigdzin (Tib. Tshe dbang Rig 'dzin), all achieved this level of realization. Guru Padmasabhava and Vimalamitra of the Buddhist Dzogchen tradition are also said to have achieved this level of realization. The second type of Rainbow Body is when the practitioner's body dissolves into the rainbow light of the essence of the five elements at the time of death without leaving any physical remains behind. This level of realization is sometimes called the Light Body or Luminous Body (Tib. 'od sku, 'od lus). The third level is when the practitioner's body shrinks at the time of death until ultimately only hair and nails are left; these are considered to be external to the body as pain is not felt when they are cut. Sometimes practitioners do not attain full dissolution into the essence of the elements and their body shrinks to a greater or lesser extent. In such cases, although the practitioner has a high level of realization, he or she has not quite completed Thögal (Tib. thod rgal) practice during their lifetime.

[28] Tib. sems nyid.

[29] Respectively Tib. bon nyid dbyings kyi sku – Body of the Ultimate Nature of Phenomena, Skt. Dharmakaya; Tib. longs pyod rdzogs pa'i sku – Body of Perfect Enjoyment, Skt. Sambhogakaya; Tib. cir yang prul p'i sku – Body of Manifold Multipurpose Emanation, Skt. Nirmanakaya. (English rendering by Khenpo Tenpa Yungdrung). The actual meaning of Sanggye, Tib. sangs rgyas, a Bönpo term for Buddha, is 'attained complete purification'(after Geshe Gelek Jinpa).

[30] Tib. g.yung drung bon, bon gsar ma, rnying ma.

[31] Tib. kun gzhi.

ways in that it does not rely on consciousness or mind in order to achieve the state of Sanggye. The characteristic method of Dzogchen is self-liberation or effortless direct insight into the Nature of Mind which is the Source of All, the ultimate and most powerful purifier of all obscurations and delusions of body, speech and mind.[32] By recognizing the difference between the ordinary mind and the Nature of Mind, and by remaining in that Natural State[33] without following thought or any movements of the mind, a Dzogchen practitioner lets all mental poisons, obscurations and impure visions dissolve back to their source, thereby eventually achieving final Buddhahood. This realization of Dzogchen can be achieved within one lifetime if one has high capacity or within three lifetimes if one's capacity is lower. This is much faster than Sutra where realization is achieved in Three Unlimited Times,[34] many *kalpa*[35] or cosmic cycles of creation and destruction, and faster than Tantra where it can take up to seven lifetimes.[36]

So Dzogchen may appear to be a kind of 'shortcut' to Buddhahood. It may sound straightforward and attractive but despite the fact that Dzogchen is called an 'effortless' path, one vital point must not be overlooked, namely the difference between Dzogchen and Dzogchen-*pa*, or between the Nature of Mind and a practitioner of Dzogchen. Dzogchen is the Great Perfection. That means all paths and fruits of other vehicles are automatically perfected within it. Thus from the point of view[37] of Dzogchen or Changchub Sem[38] – the Mind of Bodhichitta – there is no need to practise Refuge, Bodhichitta, Compassion and so on separately as these are realized spontaneously in the Natural State of Dzogchen. This is known as the 'view from the Base'.

Over the years Yongdzin Rinpoche has persistently explained that students must realize the difference between 'Dzogchen' and

---

[32] For an explanation on the differences in view and result in the various levels of Sutra, Tantra and Dzogchen see Namdak, Lopön Tenzin. Trnscr. & ed. John Myrdhin Reynolds, *Bonpo Dzogchen Teachings*, (Kathmandu: Vajra Publications, 2006).
[33] Tib. gnas lugs.
[34] Tib. grangs med pa gsum.
[35] Tib. bskal pa.
[36] According to Namdak, Yongdzin Lopön Tenzin Rinpoche, *Namkha Truldzö: the Commentary on the Precious Oral transmission of the Great Perfection which is called the Treasury of Space*, Shenten Dargye Ling, 23 July – 11 August 2006, Trnscr. & ed. Carol Ermakova and Dmitry Ermakov (Blou, Shenten Dargye Ling, 2006), *Week II*, p. 15.
[37] Tib. lta ba.
[38] Tib. byang chub sems.

'Dzogchen-*pa*' in order not to fall into the mistaken view of nihilism, the belief that since Dzogchen is the Supreme Source a Dzogchen practitioner doesn't need to engage in virtuous actions and so on, and can even manifest all sorts of erratic or negative conduct – 'anything goes'. This sort of view has nothing to do with real Dzogchen. Dzogchen-*pa* is not Dzogchen. Dzogchen-*pa* is the practitioner who tries to purify his or her obscurations by following Dzogchen methods. Hence at all times one must be aware of one's own level of realization.

Many of us have read or heard stories of realized Dzogchen yogis or Mahasiddhas who behaved very strangely and often seemingly incongruently, going beyond the social norms of 'acceptable'. Some may try to emulate this kind of behaviour or so-called Crazy Wisdom without realizing that the underlying base behind it is the complete realization of the Natural State, the ability to remain in it at all times of day and night while engaging in any kind of activity of body, speech or mind. Until this capacity is reached, merely emulating the external facets of Crazy Wisdom conduct without realizing the inner background is extremely negative and will lead to the accumulation of a vast store of negative karma rather than its purification. A Dzogchen-*pa,* then, must soberly know his or her own capacity. If one is unable to remain in the Natural State at all times then one must perform virtuous actions, accumulate merits and use any methods needed in addition to practice sessions where one is immersed in the contemplation of the Natural State. Gradually, as one's capacity increases, one will naturally be able to integrate any kind of activity with one's realization of the Nature of Mind and so conduct will change automatically without any effort. This is called the 'view of the practitioner' and is a very important point to remember while reading this book.

The Lineage

In order to understand the uniqueness of the *Zhang Zhung Nyengyud* and the tremendous importance of its Single Lineage, we should take a quick glance at the origins of this most revered Bönpo Dzogchen cycle. Originating from Kuntu Zangpo, the Mind to Mind Transmission beyond words passed through the Nine Dersheg-Buddhas:[39]

---

[39] Tib. bder gshegs dgongs brgyud.

1. Yenyi Tonpa (Bönku Kuntu Zangpo)
2. Thugjei Tonpa (Dzogku Shenlha Ökar)
3. Trulpai Tonpa (Shenrab Chenpo)
4. Rigpai Tonpa (Tseme Öden)
5. Trulshen Nangden
6. Barnang Khujyug
7. Zangza Ringtsün (Sherab Jamma)
8. Chimey Tsugphü
9. Sangwa Düpa[40]

It is important to note that, according to Yongdzin Rinpoche, the Bönku, Trülku and Dzogku Dersheg-Buddhas at the beginning of this lineage all represent the three aspects of Tonpa Shenrab Miwo, the founder of Yungdrung Bön and the origin of this *Zhang Zhung Nyengyud* cycle of Dzogchen. Thus Kuntu Zangpo, Shenlha Ökar and Shenrab Chenpo are not some abstract, general spiritual entities similar to the notion of the Judeo-Christian-Islamic God but represent respectively Body, Speech and Mind of the Bönpo Buddha Shenrab Miwo. Tseme Öden is an emanation of Tonpa Shenrab. Trulshen Nangden and Zangza Ringtsün (Sherab Jamma, Loving Goddess of Wisdom, comparable to the Buddhist Prajnaparamita) are parents of Chimey Tsugphü, the emanation of Tonpa Shenrab in the realm of the gods before his incarnation on this earth. Barnang Khujyug, also a form of Shenrab Miwo, manifested as a blue celestial cuckoo and landed on the shoulder of Zangza Ringtsün while she was taking a bath, thus producing an immaculate conception which resulted in the birth of the above-mentioned Chimey Tsugphü. Sangwa Düpa, the last Dersheg-Buddha in the Mind to Mind lineage, was born in Tagzig and then ascended to the heavenly realm to study the precepts of Tantra and Dzogchen under Chimey Tsugphü who was residing there. Sangwa Düpa later incarnated in India as Buddha Shakyamuni and propagated the Buddha-Dharma which in Bönpo understanding is a form of the Universal Indestructible Doctrine known as Drungmu Gyer in the language of Tagzig and Zhang Zhung, and as Yungdrung Bön in Tibetan. Therefore Bönpos revere Indian Buddhism as an

---

[40] Tib. Ye nyid kyi Tonpa, Bon sku Kun tu bZang po;
Thug rje'i sTon pa, rDzogs ku gShen lha 'Od dkar;
sPrul pa'i ston pa, gShen rab Chen po;
Rig pa'i sTon pa, Tshad med 'Od ldan;
'Phrul gshen sNang ldan;
Bar snang Khu byug;
bZang za Ring btsun, Shes rab Byams ma;
'Chi med gTsug phud;
gSang ba 'Dus pa.

authentic teaching concordant with the tenets of their own tradition. When asked in Amsterdam in 1995 why then Bönpos didn't practise Indian Buddhism, Yongdzin Rinpoche replied that it is because Yungdrung Bön itself is so vast that practising and preserving it leaves time for little else. Despite being very busy with this mammoth task, Yongdzin Rinpoche has himself studied tenets of various Schools of Tibetan Buddhism, in particular works of Longchen Rabjyampa[41] whom he holds in high regard:

> The text of the *Zhang zhung snyan rgyud* is like the words of an old man speaking directly. There are not many explanations or examples. Other texts, such as *Nam mkha' 'phrul mdzod* or *Yang rtse klong chen*, use very beautiful words, like a professor explaining something.
>
> My feeling is that [the works of] Longchen Rabjyampa are [in] the same [style as *Zhang zhung snyan rgyud*], [the language] is similar, and the meaning is the same, too. It is beyond thoughts it is very essential, very essential. He has described everything [about the Natural State] very clearly in the Seven Treasures,[42] in the second volume of the Treasury of the Great Vehicle.[43] This is the first text in that second volume, it is very good. Everything is explained not as precisely as in *Nam mkha' 'phrul mdzod*, *Yang rtse klong chen* or *Zhang zhung snyan rgyud*, but it goes to the meaning. The system is different, there are additions here and there, it doesn't explain and comment on the points in precisely [the same way] but the real meaning is the same.[44]

On many occasions Yongdzin Rinpoche has urged his students to keep an open mind and non-sectarian attitude saying that Buddhas, be they from Bönpo or Indian Buddhist lineages, are fully realized beings beyond any sectarianism and that in the real sense, Buddha is our own non-dual and totally pure Buddha-Nature. Yongdzin Rinpoche also explained that those wishing to practise the *Zhang Zhung Nyengyud* should honour their previous vows and commitments, one of the five main qualifications for the pupil.[45]

---

[41] Tib. Klong chen Rab 'byams pa.

[42] Tib. mDzod bdun.

[43] Tib. Theg mchog mdzod.

[44] Excerpt from an interview with Yongdzin Rinpoche, 31st July, 2009, Shenten Dargye Ling, Blou, France.

[45] Namdak, Yongdzin Lopön Tenzin Rinpoche. *Nyam-zhag Gom-pa'i Lag-len (lTaba spyi-gcod kyi mnyam-bzhag sgom pa'i lag-len), Shambhala Centre, Paris, April 1997,* Trnscr. & ed. Carol Ermakova and Dmitry Ermakov (Blou, Shenten Dargye Ling,

Sangwa Düpa passed the transmission on to Lhabön Yongsu Dagpa who lived in the realm of the Lha[46] celestial gods, and thus the Lineage of the Twenty-Four Exalted Individuals[47] began. Transmission became coded in words which were transmitted from Master to disciple in utmost secrecy, whispered into the ear through a bamboo tube. What was transmitted were the *bKa' brgyud skor bzhi*, The Four Cycles of the Transmission of Precepts. These are the four cycles of the *Zhang Zhung Nyengyud*:

1. *Phyi lta ba spyi gcod* – The External cycle dealing with the general exposition of the view;
2. *Nang mang ngag dmar khrid* – The Inner cycle containing oral instructions of the vital points;
3. *gSang ba rig pa gcer mthong* – The Secret cycle introducing naked Rigpa[48] or Self-Awareness;
4. *Yang gsang gnas lugs phugs chod* – The Exceedingly secret cycle which brings certainty regarding the Natural State as the Source of All.[49]

Lhabön Yongsu Dagpa transmitted the teaching to Lubön Banam who belonged to the race of Lu[50] water-spirits. He in turn transmitted it to Mibön Tride Zambu who was human, a native of Tagzig, an exceedingly ancient Central Asian country, cradle of Yungdrung Bön, located to the north-west of Mount Kailash, the inner region of the Zhang Zhung Confederation. Tride Zambu transmitted the teachings to Banam Kyolpo, who was a native of Zhang Zhung and the teachings remained in Zhang Zhung for many centuries where they were transmitted orally from Master to Master within the Single Lineage, hence its name *The Oral Transmission of Zhang Zhung*. This part of the lineage is called the Twenty-Four Exalted Individuals and is further divided into four sections: The Symbolic Transmission of Yungdrung Sempas,[51] The Awareness Transmission of the Rigdzins,[52] The Oral Transmission of the Exalted Individuals[53] and The Transmission of the Bright Scholars.[54]

2006), pp. 1-2.
[46] Tib. lha.
[47] Tib. gang zag nyi shu rtsa bzhi.
[48] Tib. rig pa.
[49] For a full list of the texts within each of the Four Cycles see Reynolds, *The Oral Transmission from Zhang Zhung*, pp. 197-203.
[50] Tib. klu; Skt. Naga.
[51] Tib. sems dpa' brda'u brgyud. Tib. g.yung drung sems dpa' corresponds to Bodhisattva of the Indian Buddhist system.
[52] Tib. rig 'dzin rig pa'i brgyud pa.
[53] Tib. gang zag snyan khungs kyi brgyud pa.

The last of the Twenty-Four Masters was Tsepung Dawa Gyaltsen. He transmitted the teachings to Tapihritsa who practised in solitude for nine years and attained the Rainbow Body of Great Transfer[55] in the same way as all the preceding Masters of the *Zhang Zhung Nyengyud* had.

This twenty-fifth Master is of paramount importance to the *Oral Tradition of Zhang Zhung* because after realizing Rainbow Body he took the form of a small boy, a Trülku, to teach Gurub Nangzher Lödpo, the royal priest of the last Zhang Zhung king Ligmincha. It was Tapihritsa who allowed the *Four Cycles of Precepts* to be written down. It was also Tapihritsa who permitted this lineage to be taught to more than one student at a time, thereby allowing the teachings to spread more widely. He did this in response to the unstable and dangerous situation which was developing for Yungdrung Bön in Tibet. Tibet's king, Trisong Deutsen, had decided to favour Indian Buddhism over Yungdrung Bön for political reasons and launched a persecution of Yungdrung Bön in 749 AD.[56] Furthermore, Tibet was bent on the conquest of Zhang Zhung itself so Yungdrung Bön came under threat there, too. Through treason and trickery, Trisong Deutsen's agents succeeded in ambushing and killing the king Ligmincha, and Zhang Zhung fell into chaos. Paradoxically however, it was the killing of Ligmincha and the collapse of Zhang Zhung that saved Yungdrung Bön from total annihilation both in Tibet and in Zhang Zhung itself. As we have seen, Gurub Nangzher Lödpo was royal priest to the king Ligmincha. Besides being a Dzogchen-*pa* he was also a highly accomplished Tantric yogi possessing great magical powers which he obtained through the practice of his *yidam*[57] Zhang Zhung Meri,[58] an extremely wrathful form of the Tantric deity

---

[54] Tib. mkhas pa lo pan gyi brgyud pa.

[55] Tib. 'ja' lus pho ba chen po.

[56] According to traditional Bönpo *bsTan rtsis* chronology. Samten Karmay gives between 780–790 AD as the date for persecution. See Karmay, Samten G. *The Treasury of Good Sayings* (Delhi: Motilal Banarsidass Publishers Private Limited, 1972), Introduction, p.xxxii.

[57] Tib. yid dam; a manifestation of Buddha in the form of the deity which is used as the primary means for obtaining realization. The Bönpo understanding of *yidam* is not limited to a Tantric deity as is often the case in Buddhism; the supreme *yidam* of Bön is the Natural State of Mind although even a text or prayer can be referred to as *yidam* if used as a primary practice. It is sometimes translated into English as 'tutelary deity'. Generally, Bönpo Tantric *yidams* are different forms of Tonpa Shenrab Miwo which he assumed while performing different activities for the propagation of Yungdrung Bön.

[58] Tib. zhang zhung me ri.

Walchen Gekhöd.[59] At the request of Ligmincha's bereaved queen, Nangzher Lödpo dispatched a golden *dzwo* missile to Tibet mortally wounding the Tibetan king. Realizing where it came from, the king sent a hundred horsemen to Zhang Zhung to find Nangzher Lödpo and negotiate with him for their king's life. They found the Master on an island on Lake Darog[60] and asked him for terms. He agreed to lift the magic from the king on three conditions:

1. A large golden shrine should be built to entomb the remains of Zhang Zhung's king Ligmincha;

2. The people of Nangzher Lödpo's Gurub clan should be exempt from Tibetan government taxes and should have privileges at the Tibetan court;

3. None of the 360 types of Yungdrung Bön teachings practised and taught by Gyerpung Nangzher Lödpo should be suppressed in any way.

The Tibetans had no option but to agree and so Gyerpung Nangzher Lödpo went to Tibet and lifted the curse from the king. Since *Zhang Zhung Nyengyud* Dzogchen was Nangzher Lödpo's primary practice, it was neither suppressed, destroyed nor hidden as a *terma* or treasure text. Furthermore, seeing how many disturbances there were in his time and how many there would be in the future, Gyerpung Nangzher Lödpo searched for powerful spiritual beings whom he could charge with the task of protecting this Oral Tradition. Through his magical powers he subdued two potent, ancient spiritual beings and put them under oath: the mighty sky-god Werro Nyipangse[61] who was worshipped not only in Zhang Zhung but also under different names in Central and Inner Asia, the Great Steppe, Siberia and Tibet,[62] and his consort, the goddess Menmo Kumaradza.[63] Since the eighth century these two gods have been inseparably linked to the transmission of the *Zhang Zhung Nyengyud*, protecting its integrity and its practitioners.

Although Tapihritsa allowed Nangzher Lödpo to teach the *Zhang Zhung Nyengyud* to larger groups of students due to the changing times and in order to benefit more beings, the Single Lineage transmission – the very heart of this Dzogchen cycle – remained secret, passing from Master to a single disciple and,

---

[59] Tib. dbal chen ge khod.

[60] Tib. da rog mtsho.

[61] Tib. wer ro nyi pang sad.

[62] For a study of how Nyipangse is connected with the pantheons of gods of other ancient religions of Eurasia see Ermakov, *Bo and Bön*, pp. 251-309.

[63] Tib. sman mo ku ma ra dza.

unbroken to this day, is currently held by Yongdzin Lopön Tenzin Namdak Rinpoche.

Lineage Tree

Gyerpung Nangzher Lödpo is important for another reason, too. He unified in himself all the lineages of the *Zhang Zhung Nyengyud*. The lineage we have been discussing so far is known as the Uninterrupted Lineage,[64] so called because all the Masters in this lineage followed one after the other with no chronological breaks. However, there was also an Interrupted Lineage[65] which had several branches. This lineage is known as 'interrupted' not because it was actually interrupted but because gaps appeared in the chronology of the Masters when the oral tradition was written down. This is how Pa Tengyal Zangpo, the compiler of the life-stories of the Masters explains this:

> [...] there does not exist a total chronology for the transmission of the above instructions. Well then, it might be objected, if there does not exist an original source for the transmission of these instructions, how then may this be distinguished as Bon? The original source of any transmission is exceedingly important! We answer that, with regard to this original source, it was transmitted from Horti Chenpo (who is a reliable source). So, this transmission which has become divided and fragmented, still has a single root (which is the great Horti). For the reason (that it has become fragmented), it is called "the discontinuous transmission."[66]

There were three branches of the Interrupted Lineage which came directly to the Drubthob-Mahasiddhas of Zhang Zhung from three different Dersheg-Buddhas of the Mind to Mind Lineage (Chimey Tsugphü, Yeshen Tsugphü[67] and Sangwa Düpa). All three branches came together with the Uninterrupted Lineage in Gurub Nangzher Lödpo.

Zhang Zhung Garab and Garab Dorje

In the branch of the Interrupted Lineage stemming from Sangwa Düpa we find a very interesting figure, a Master known as Zhang Zhung

---

[64] Tib. rgyud pa 'khrug med.

[65] Tib. rgyud pa 'khrug can.

[66] Reynolds, *The Oral Tradition* p. 68.

[67] According to Yongdzin Lopön Tenzin Namdak, although Yeshen Tsugphü does not appear among the line of the Nine Dershegs, he is a Buddha and has a direct lineage from Kuntu Zangpo.

Garab. Several leading scholars of Bön such as Yongdzin Lopön Tenzin Namdak, Samten G. Karmay and John M. Reynolds have suggested that this Master might be identical with Garab Dorje of the Nyingma Dzogchen lineage.[68] It may be then, that both Tibetan lineages of Dzogchen have a single root not only in terms of their ultimate source, Bönku/Dharmakaya, but also in terms of lineage. Both lineages came from Central Asia to Tibet via different countries, with the Nyingma lineage tracing its origin to Oddiyana[69] and the Bönpo lineage coming to Tibet from Zhang Zhung. Oddiyana and Zhang Zhung were neighbouring countries and their borders were vague, not like in our modern times. Several Bönpo Drubthob-Mahasiddhas such as Drenpa Namkha, Tsewang Rigdzin,[70] Pema Thongdrol[71] and others travelled back and forth between Zhang Zhung and Oddiyana; furthermore there is a Cycle of Indian Bön.[72] So Garab Dorje and Zhang Zhung Garab may indeed be the same person. This hypothesis is further supported by the fact that Bönpo and Nyingma Dzogchen do not differ in terms of their base, path, view, or result. All this, then, suggests a common source.

There is also later textual evidence which connects Garab Dorje with Bönpo Dzogchen. For example, in the text the *Golden Spoon*[73] rediscovered by the great *terton*[74] Yungdrung Lingpa[75] we read:

> Vairotsana was sitting in the Tiger's Nest[76] in Bhutan. When he was practising in the cave there one night, the cave became filled with light, the earth trembled and emitted sounds like a dragon roaring. Vairotsana looked in front of him and in a rainbow circle he saw Drenpa Namkha[77] with his two sons;[78] they appeared directly to him.

[68] Oral communication from Yongdzin Lopön Tenzin Namdak; Karmay, *The Little Luminous Boy*, p. 7; Reynolds, *The Oral Tradition*, p. 59; John Myrdhin Reynolds, *The Golden Letters*, (Ithaca, New York: Snow Lion Publications, 1996), p. 227.

[69] Tib. U rgyan.

[70] Tib. Tshe dbang Rig 'dzin.

[71] Tib. Pad ma mThong grol.

[72] Tib. rgya gar bon skor. For more information on Bön of India see Ermakov, *Bo and Bön*, pp. 23, 205-206.

[73] Tib. rDzogs chen gser thur ma lo rgyus spyi ching chen mo gab pa 'byed pa'i lde mig zhes bya ba bzhugs.

[74] Tib. gter ton – Spiritual Treasure Discoverer.

[75] Tib.g.Yung drung gLing pa alias Tib. rDor rje gLing pa (1346-1405) was one of several *tertons* who found both Bönpo and Nyingma *termas*.

[76] Tib. sPa gro stag tshang.

[77] This is the second Drenpa Namkha, the prince of Zhang Zhung. See footnote 16.

[78] I.e. Tsewang Rigdzin and Pema Thongdrol just mentioned above.

Drenpa Namkha was white in colour and decorated with the six bone ornaments. In his right hand he was holding up a swastika which was spinning by his head. In his left hand he was holding a skull cup filled with blood. Under his arm he was holding a trident decorated with semiprecious and precious stones as well as with various silk drapes. He was in a dancing posture, and he was moving.

His son, Tsewang Rigdzin, was a darkish white colour. All his ornaments and decorations were perfect and Vairotsana saw him clearly. He felt devotion to him at that time.

This teaching was written in gold and kept inside a gold reliquary box. Drenpa Namkha touched Vairotsana's forehead, neck and chest with it and gave him the four empowerments.

He gave him the three important points of teaching and also advice.

He said:
'Ho!

Boy of awareness, spiritual son! Do not be deluded! Listen to me!
I am Garab Dorje,
I am Drenpa Namkha
I am Lhagod Thoglebar,[79]
I am Namkha Yungdrung,[80]
I am also Drugse, Chemchog Kagying.[81]
I show a Bönku form.
To whoever is devoted to me, I will appear as Sambhogakaya,
Impure beings will see me as Nirmanakaya.
I am the King of the Quintessence of the Three Kayas.
I am also the Free Life, Lachen Drenpa, the great lama of Namkha.

This is the essence of the Ultimate Vehicle of Bön. This is the drops of nectar from the golden spoon.
Practise and then hide this as a treasure.'
And then he gave the teachings to Vairotsana. Vairotsana hid it in the Tiger's Nest.[82]

Tapihritsa is also said to have been one of the emanations of Drenpa Namkha[83] so this brings us back to *Zhang Zhung Nyengyud Dzogchen*.

---

[79] Tib. Lha rgod thog las 'bar.
[80] Tib. Nam mkha' g.Yung drung.
[81] Tib, 'Brug gsas Chem pa, Che mchog mKha' gying.
[82] Bönpo Tengyur, vol. 295, p. 23. Kindly translated by Yongdzin Rinpoche, 07.08.09, Shenten Dargye Ling, France.
[83] Oral communication from Yongdzin Rinpoche.

A Mongol Connection

The Interrupted Lineage coming from Chimey Tsugphü contains two other interesting figures: Sumpai Bönpo Awadong and Gya Yi Bönpo Salwa Öchen. The former was of proto-Mongol stock and received the transmission from Lama Rasang Trinnekö who comes eleventh in the line of this lineage. Sumpai Awadong's student Salwa Öchen was Chinese. These two Masters went to their home countries and spread the teachings of *Zhang Zhung Nyengyud* Dzogchen there but we have no direct information on the fate of the ensuing lineages. However, we do know that both of them realized Rainbow Body in the same manner as their teacher.[84]

Sumpai Awadong was from a country the Tibetans call Sumpa.[85] It has been suggested that Sumpa peoples correspond to the Syanbi (Xianbei) who comprised several nomadic states in that vast region over the course of history. The first and most powerful of those was Sumbe Uuls which was established by the Syanbi leader Tanshihai during the Syanbi military campaign of 168-173 AD in which they won control from the Hunnu[86] over the Great Steppe, Lake Kokonoor and part of what is now known as the Amdo region of Tibet. The Sumbe Empire lasted until the beginning of the fourth century AD when it split into several Syanbi states, namely Toba (Tabgach), Muyung, Tuyuhun (Togon) as well as Former Yan, Later Yan and Southern Yan. All these states, some of which controlled considerable parts of north-western China and modern day Amdo, were governed by offshoots of the Syanbi royal and noble clans. The longest surviving Syanbi state was Tuyuhun, which is known in Tibet as Azha. They held on as a state until 633 AD when they were invaded and lost their lands, with one part annexed by Srongtsen Gampo to become the Amdo province of Tibet and another taken over by the Tang Chinese. There was also Sumpa in east Tibet near Khyungpo[87] in Kham, which I believe was another Syanbi settlement. Sumpai Awadong, then, could have been a native of any of these territories although it is likely he was from Sumbe or one of the succeeding Syanbi states because he is described as Sogpo,[88] the name Tibetans use for proto-Mongols and later Mongols.

An interesting link suggesting that the *Zhang Zhung*

---

[84] Karmay, *The Treasury of Good Sayings*, p. 54.
[85] Tib. sum pa. For interactions of Sumbe/Sumpa to Zhang Zhung and Tibet see Ermakov, *Bo and Bön*, pp. 25-26, 68-70, 731-736.
[86] Often spelt Hsiung-nu or Xiongnu.
[87] Tib. khyung po.
[88] Tib. sog po.

Nyamgyud teachings of Sumpai Awadong may have survived until recently is found among the Buryat-Mongols of Southern Siberia in the great Master Sode Lama (1846-1916). Sode Lama lived in the Barguzin region of north-east Buryatia and is venerated in those parts as he combined without conflict practices of the Buryatian branch of Gelugpa Buddhism with the native Bө Murgel tradition.[89] During his life he displayed considerable magical powers and his death was remarkable, too. Although he asked to be left alone in a *shalash* twigtent in the *taiga* forest for nine days to die, his main student was overcome by doubt and opened the tent after seven days, only to discover that Sode Lama's body had shrunk to the size of a baby. This matches the descriptions of the way in which Dzogchen Masters in Tibet attained Rainbow Body. According to the village elders – simple non-Buddhist folk who know nothing about Dzogchen or the specific fruit of its realization – Sode Lama's father and grandfather died in the same way and indeed, they left no bodies at all. While Sode Lama took up Buddhist practice and became a lama, his father and grandfather had nothing to do with Buddhism. They were 100% Bө priests of the Bө Murgel religion. Since Gelugpa Buddhism has no Dzogchen lineage as such[90] and because Sode Lama's father and grandfather were not connected with Buddhism at all, the only plausible explanation for this can be that some lineage of Bönpo Dzogchen, possibly the *Zhang Zhung Nyengyud* lineage coming from Sumpai Awadong, may have survived in Buryatia until the beginning of the 20th century (Sode Lama did not pass it on).[91] If that is the case then the geographical spread of Bönpo Dzogchen was much wider than previously thought.

Experiential Transmission

Parallel to the transmission of the *Four Cycles of Precepts* mentioned above, *Zhang Zhung Nyengyud* Dzogchen has another system of transmission which is known as the Experiential Transmission or the *Nyamgyud*.[92] The *Nyamgyud* consists of the last testaments of the

---

[89] The spiritual tradition of Mongol-Buryats which shares many features with Tib. gdod mai bon, often referred to as Tengrism and placed within the larger context of Siberian Shamanism. For an extensive study on the parallels and difference between Bön and Bө Murgel, see Ermakov, *Bө and Bön.*

[90] Although the Fifth Dalai Lama received Dzogchen teachings and wrote his own treatise on Dzogchen entitled *gSang ba rgya can,* it was never widely spread within the Gelugpa School and those who practised it did not attain Rainbow Body.

[91] See Ermakov, *Bө and Bön,* pp. 736-740.

[92] Tib. nyams rgyud.

Masters of the Single Lineage, the quintessential personal instructions summarizing their realizations which are imparted to their heart disciples, next in the line of Masters. The further the lineage went in time, the more testaments there were. For a long time the *Nyamgyud* lineage of transmission ran parallel with the *Kagyud*,[93] the main corpus of the cycle. However, the thirty-second Master, Pönchen Tsenpo (a very important figure in this tradition as he translated the *Zhang Zhung Nyengyud* from the language of Zhang Zhung into Tibetan), taught the *Nyamgyud* and the *Kagyud* to different disciples. Pönchen Tsenpo taught the *Nyamgyud* to Pönchen Lhundrub Muthur from whom the line went to Shengyal Lhatse, Lhagom Karpo, Ngodrub Gyaltsen Ringmo and Orgom Kundul. This lineage became known as the Lower Transmission[94] because it was transmitted by Pönchen Tsenpo in Lower Zhang Zhung (modern North-West Tibet) and it is the teachings which passed through this lineage which are presented here.

We should focus our attention for a moment on Shengyal Lhatse, not only because of the colourful story which brought him into contact with this lineage, but also because of his relationship with the tenth century Nyingma Master Zurpoche Shakya Jungne.[95] This Master came to see Shengyal Lhatse at his Yungdrung Lhatse[96] hermitage near Lake Dangra[97] and requested Dzogchen teachings. Shengyal Lhatse agreed and taught him the *Nyamgyud*. The two Masters became very close friends. Later, Zurchen asked Shengyal Lhatse whether he could write down the instructions he had received from him, but as rumours had begun circulating among the Buddhists that he had converted to Bön, he asked whether he could change little things such as replacing the word Bön with Chö[98] and so on to make it acceptable to Buddhists. Shengyal Lhatse permitted him to change some names but not the meaning, and so Pönchen Tsenpo's and Shengyal Lhatse's oral instructions flowed into the Nyingma School of Tibetan Buddhism under the title *Rig pa'i khu byug*, The Cuckoo of

---

[93] Tib. bka' rgyud.
[94] Tib. smad rgyud.
[95] Tib. Zur po che Shakya 'Byung gnas.
[96] Tib. g.Yund drung lha rtse.
[97] Tib. Dang ra g.yu mtsho.
[98] Tib. chos. Although this word is an original Bönpo term which in early Bönpo contexts refers to ritual traditions, when Buddhism was introduced in the 8th century AD this word was used to translate the Sanskrit word *dharma* and so it came to mean 'buddhism'.

Self-Awareness,[99] so called in honour of Pönchen Tsenpo who transformed into a cuckoo at the end of his life and flew away into the dimension of Bönku.

Having transmitted the *Nyamgyud* to Tibetan disciples, Pönchen Tsenpo travelled to Gughe and Purang in Upper Zhang Zhung (modern South-West Tibet). There he imparted the *Kagyud* to Guge Sherab Loden from whom the lineage went to Purang Kunga Ringmo, Naljyor Sechog, Khyungjyid Muthur, Tsi Dewa Ringmo and Thogme Zhigpo. This lineage became known as the Upper Transmission.[100] Both lineages came together in Yangton Sherab Gyaltsen and it is he who, with the permission of Orgom Kundul, wrote down the *Nyamgyud*, which until then had been an entirely oral transmission.

Modern day Transmission

Since we are fortunate to have John M. Reynold's *The Oral Tradition from Zhang-Zhung* which deals in great detail with the history of the lineages of the *Zhang Zhung Nyengyud*, the reader is referred there for information on the other branches and further history. Here it will suffice to say that these lineages have safely arrived to Yongdzin Lopön Tenzin Namdak Rinpoche who is the current lineage holder of this tradition. He received the complete lineage from his Master Yongdzin Lopön Sangye Tenzin (died 1977) and it is thanks to these two Masters that the *Zhang Zhung Nyengyud* has been taught more widely, eventually becoming available to Western students.[101]

Yongdzin Lopön Sanggye Tenzin and Yongdzin Lopön Tenzin Namdak found themselves in a situation not that dissimilar to the persecution of Yungdrung Bön in the eighth century; their country was overthrown and occupied by Communists who systematically and brutally destroyed both Bönpo and Buddhist monasteries, lay communities, religious objects and sacred texts, while practitioners were killed or imprisoned. Both these extraordinary Lopöns were faced with the enormous task of trying to save, preserve and pass on their vast Yungdrung Bön traditions. It is in this atmosphere of uncertainty that the chief guardian of Yungdrung Bön in general and

---

[99] Namdak, Yongdzin Lopön Tenzin Rinpoche. *Dringpo Sorzhag, Chapter II: The Clothes, Pith Instructions of Zhang Zhung Nyen Gyud Masters, Blanc, 15th – 17th September 2002*, Trnscr. & ed. Carol Ermakova and Dmitry Ermakov (Blou, Shenten Dargye Ling, 2006), p. 69.

[100] Tib.stod rgyud.

[101] For the complete lineage tree of the *Zhang Zhung Nyengyud* see the diagram on page no.36.

of the *Zhang Zhung Nyengyud* in particular, Machog Sidpai Gyalmo,[102] appeared to Yongdzin Lopön Sangye Tenzin and instructed him to start teaching the *Zhang Zhung Nyengyud* more openly. Otherwise, she said, this tradition would soon come to an end. Before the Chinese takeover of Tibet, the *Zhang Zhung Nyengyud* – like most other Dzogchen cycles – was normally taught to a very small number of students. However, with the Chinese invasion the situation radically changed, requiring adjustments in the way teachings are transmitted and preserved. The *Zhang Zhung Nyengyud* was transmitted more widely, initially amongst Bönpo monks and some Tibetan laymen until, in 1989, Yongdzin Lopön Tenzin Namdak Rinpoche brought it to the West when he visited England (Devon), Italy and the USA at the invitation of the Dzogchen Community founded by Chögyal Namkhai Norbu.[103] Since then Yongdzin Rinpoche has visited many countries to teach the *Zhang Zhung Nyengyud* and other Bönpo Dzogchen cycles to many students. An international group of followers gradually grew, creating the need for a place where these teachings can be transmitted and preserved in the West. In 2005 Shenten Dargye Ling, Yongdzin Rinpoche's international Yungdrung Bön centre, was established in France; teaching and practice retreats are held there regularly.

---

[102] Tib. Ma mchog Srid pa'i rGyal mo.
[103] Tib. Chos rgyal Nam mkha'i Nor bu.

Lineage Tree Diagram

Note on editing

Realizing the preciousness of these teachings given in the West in English, my wife Carol and I set about transcribing them for use within the Bönpo community. Following Yongdzin Rinpoche's encouragement and instructions, repetitions are edited and grammar irregularities are evened out. The unmistakable, clear voice of this great Master, however, still speaks through the written texts. In the case of *Masters of the Zhang Zhung Nyengyud*, Yongdzin Rinpoche chose to publish the edited transcript as a public book, making these valuable and rare teachings available to all. Some lamas or practitioners may query this, considering such a publication inappropriate for such heart teachings and indeed, similar reservations were voiced by some when *Heart Drops of Dharmakaya*[104] was published. It contains teachings by Yongdzin Rinpoche on *'Od gsal rdzogs pa chen po'i lam gyi rim pa khrid yig kun tu bzang po'i snying tig shes bya ba zhugs*, a Dzogchen practice manual by Shardza Tashi Gyaltsen[105] dealing with all aspects of Dzogchen practice from special

[104] Gyaltsen, Shardza Tashi. Commentary by Lopön Tenzin Namdak, *Heart Drops of Dharmakaya: Dzogchen Practice of the Bön Tradition* (Ithaca: Snow Lion Publications, 1993).

[105] Shardza Tashi Gyaltsen also received and practised teachings of the *Zhang Zhung Nyengyud* and that is why he is included in the lineage tree diagram. However, at the moment it is not clear precisely how the lineage came to him and more research needs to be done on this. Nevertheless, even now we know he received different parts of the *Zhang Zhung Nyengyud* from different Masters such as Tib. mChog sprul Nyi ma 'Od zer and Tib. Shes rab g.Yung drung the 25th Abbott of Menri Monastery of the Southern Lineage (see lineage tree diagram above). Born in 1859 in Dzakhog (Tib. rdza khog) in Kham, Shardza Tashi Gyaltsen became a Bönpo monk at the age of nine. He received a great number of teachings and initiations on the levels Dö, Gyud and Dzogchen from twenty-four of his main teachers and other lamas. At the age of thirty-four he retired to a hermitage in Yungdrung Lhunpo (Tib. g.Yung drung lhun po) and practised all the teachings he had received very intensely. Besides being a great practitioner he was also a great scholar and prolific writer, clarifying many points of Dzogchen practice in his books such as the above-mentioned Tib. *Kun bzang snying tig, sKu gsum rang shar* and *Byings rig mdzod*. Through the breadth of his knowledge and strength of his realization he became a spiritual magnet attracting many students not only Bönpo but also Buddhist from various Schools including Gelugpa, and become involved in what is known as Rime (Tib. ris med) or the non-sectarian movement in Eastern Tibet. While holding the ancient Yungdrung Bön transmissions in their purity, Shardza Tashi Gyaltsen also created his own unique way of practice and at the end of his life he realized Rainbow Body in 1935. Some of his students subsequently realized Rainbow Bodies under the extremely difficult circumstances of the Chinese takeover of Tibet and the Cultural Revolution (for detailed accounts of this see *Heart Drops of Dharmakaya* pp. 135-137). The strength of the Bönpo Dzogchen lineage in general and of the *Zhang Zhung Nyengyud* in particular has not diminished and those who follow it continue to manifest the highest

Dzogchen Preliminaries to Trekchö, Thögal and Bardo[106] teachings. On that occasion I asked Yongdzin Rinpoche why he gave his blessing to publish such an esoteric text so publicly and whether it might cause some damage for those who are not prepared for such high teachings. He replied that:

- Firstly, the guardians of Bönpo Dzogchen have ordered the Masters to teach it openly;
- Secondly, Dzogchen teachings are an 'open secret' i.e. if one has no capacity then one will not be able to understand them and will not be interested in reading;
- Thirdly, for those who have capacity and connection, it may bring great benefit by providing a link to the text and Master which they can then follow if they wish to enter the way of Dzogchen;
- Fourthly, it is clearly stated in the text that if one wishes to put these teachings into practice then just reading the book is not enough; one must find and follow an authentic Master.

Because of these points, he said, the publication of *Heart Drops of Dharmakaya* was allowed and would bring benefit. This was reiterated regarding the publication of *Masters of the Zhang Zhung Nyengyud*.

Back in 1999 when these particular teachings were given, Yongdzin Rinpoche still used many Sanskrit terms more familiar to a Western audience, whereas nowadays he more commonly uses the original Tibetan Bönpo terms. In this publication some of these key terms can be found as footnotes in Wylie transliteration.

In editing the transcript we have taken the liberty of putting the final instructions of each Master alongside his picture and under his name rather than alongside his student, and have also moved certain passages relating to general topics such as Lamai Naljyor or question and answer sessions to make for easier reading. Nothing, however, has been added (except some clarifications given by Yongdzin Rinpoche himself on different occasions) or omitted; the text remains true to the words and spirit of the teachings and to Yongdzin Rinpoche's unique style of delivery in English.

Since the Dzogchen teachings of Yungdrung Bön and Buddhism are identical in essence and may even have the same

---

fruit of realization even in our modern times.

[106] Tib. khregs chod, thod rgal, bar do.

original source in prehistory, the pith instructions contained in this book can greatly benefit practitioners of both traditions. Whether you have already received Dzogchen teachings from a qualified lama or have just come into contact with Dzogchen through this or other publications, these words will inspire you and provide the means of furthering your practice. On the instruction of Yongdzin Rinpoche, we have included his explanations on the Lamai Naljyor according to the *Zhang Zhung Nyengyud*, as this is the fundamental practice of Dzogchen. However, if you are not already connected to this lineage and wish to enter into the actual practice of the *Zhang Zhung Nyengyud*, this will not suffice; you must seek a qualified lama to receive the necessary transmissions and teachings.

Dzogchen is a profound teaching so obtaining a precise understanding and clear experience of the Natural State of Mind is of paramount importance. This cannot come through reading alone, it can only be facilitated by a qualified, authentic Master who carries the blessings of the lineage.

Mutsug Marro! May all be Auspicious!

Dmitry Ermakov
Low Bishopley, UK
November 2008

རྫོགས་པ་ཆེན་པོ་ཞང་ཞུང་སྙན་རྒྱུད་ཀྱི་ཉམས་རྒྱུད་སྐྱ་རུ་བཞུགས་པ་ལེགས་སོ༎

rDzogs pa chen po zhang zhung snyan rgyud kyi nyams rgyud skya ru
bzhugs pa legs so

Teachings by Yongdzin Lopön Tenzin Namdak on

**Chyaru: The Experiential Transmission of the Oral Tradition
of the Great Perfection from Zhang Zhung**

Cergy, France, 26-28 April, 1999

Preliminary comments

First I want to explain a little bit about this text. There are four subdivisions[107] in the *Zhang Zhung Nyengyud* which were preached by the Buddha Lineage of Nine Dersheg-Buddhas and then by the Rigdzin Lineage.[108] The main text of the *Zhang Zhung Nyengyud* was taught by all of them.

Once a pupil receives instructions on these teachings, engages in the practice they explain and achieves Buddhahood or Rainbow Body, he is ready to teach the next pupil. Each pupil is taught all the texts, all four subdivisions, as well as the Master's own special experience,[109] a few final words on the condensed meaning of what he has understood. Those few final words of the condensed explanations of all the Lineage Masters comprising their special, essential teachings were put together at different times into large, medium and short collections.[110] I am reading from the long one, which is more or less the same as the others except that more words are used. So first each Master learned and practised the *Zhang Zhung Nyengyud* and then he was ready to teach. Finally, he put his own special experience into a few, final words for his pupil, and these were all collected. This is known as the Experiential Transmission.[111]

This Teaching was kept in a Single Lineage for many centuries. What does that mean? Although each Master can have many students, the Single Lineage Teaching of these final few words is only taught to one pupil who then becomes the Lineage Holder. This tradition has been kept unbroken up until now. In our difficult modern times it is permitted to teach this Experiential Transmission to a group of students, but everyone who receives it must keep it tidily and faithfully. Many can hear and benefit from this Teaching, but it is very difficult to find a suitable pupil for the Single Lineage, even today, because once a student receives the Single Lineage teachings he should disconnect himself from worldly life and devote himself to practice until he attains Buddhahood. Such a student can be recognized by various signs and qualifications, and permission to pass the lineage on to him or her must also be granted by the Guardians. All the Masters in this lineage bore many hardships as they practised to obtain Rainbow Body. In those days their biographies were not

---

[107] I.e. *bKa' brgyud skor bzhi.*

[108] Tib. grub thob snyan khung gi brgyud pa.

[109] Tib. nyams.

[110] See Introduction.

[111] Tib. nyams rgyud.

written down in detail but in fact they are very similar to that of Milarepa.[112] A lot is written about him and he is quite famous nowadays. The Masters of the *Zhang Zhung Nyengyud* all had similar experiences and suffered hardships for a long time, until they achieved Rainbow Body.

I will do my best to translate and if you have questions, check against your experience of the Nature,[113] not just against words; it is important to check this Teaching against your experience. Here we are explaining what the Natural State is and what it is like, but you should clarify this by yourself. You need to verify by yourself, otherwise if you don't have your own experience it is difficult for this to become clear to you even if you read books or listen to Teachings.

The purpose of this Teaching is to become more stable in the Natural State as you develop your practice and meditation further, thus all your defilements and obscurations are purified. That is the real purpose of religion. Even though everything is already perfect within our condition, we need to concentrate and practise. This will bring benefit for you in this lifetime, but will also forge a connection and take you to Buddhahood, so in fact it is better not to make any excuses but to practise; this is of great benefit.

Guru Yoga

At the beginning of each session you should try to remember refuge, Bodhichitta and prayers, then do Guru Yoga. I will show you the cards of the Masters and explain how to visualize each Master in the series. You should visualize them as clearly as possible. Don't just take a quick look at the picture; try to make it really clear. When you remember the Masters, don't think they are just a picture like the ones here; the form of the Master is like the one depicted here but you should vividly visualize a Master who has a body of luminous light, is endowed with knowledge and wisdom, and is completely purified.

You should visualize each Master as he appears here and

---

[112] Tib. Mi la ras pa.
[113] This does not imply any physical nature. Here Rinpoche uses this word to refer to what is often termed 'the Nature of Mind' in English. The Nature of Mind is a translation of the Tibetan term *sems nyid* which has many synonyms, such as *gnas lugs*, *rang bzhin*, *ngo bo nyid* and so on, all of which mean 'nature' in the sense of the fundamental or essential nature of being or of an individual, the nature of mind. Since Yongdzin Rinpoche gave these teachings in English, we cannot be sure which exact Tibetan term he had in mind in each instance when he used the word Nature, so we have simply left it as it is in the text.

receive his wisdom represented by the three elements which purify all defilements, then take blessings and initiation from him.

Once your visualization of the Master is clear, he sends very strong wisdom-fire from his chest. It looks like fire, but it is wisdom-fire. It reaches you and spreads through your whole body, burning not your material body but all your defilements, ignorance, emotions and obscurations. They are all burned out.

Then water comes from his chest. It is white like milk, wisdom-water which washes away all obscurations.

That is followed by wind, wisdom-wind. It is very strong and blows away all defilements which are left.

These three elements of fire, water and wind are not ordinary elements but the wisdom of a Master.

After these three have purified your body, speech and mind, you are ready to receive blessings and knowledge from the Master's Body, Speech and Mind. A white syllable **A** emanates from the Master's crown-chakra and dissolves into your crown-chakra. A red syllable **Om** emanates from his throat-chakra and dissolves into your throat chakra and a blue syllable **Hung** emanates from his heart chakra and dissolves into your heart-chakra. This is an initiation. Real initiation depends only on your devotion and visualization. Otherwise, if you just look at the pictures of the Masters but nothing changes for you afterwards, you may think that you have received some initiation, but in fact you haven't received anything at all. Everything depends on your devotion. Your devotion may be clear and strong for the moment but it may soon disappear; if your devotion doesn't last long then the initiation can't last, either. That is why it is better to maintain strong faith in these Masters and the Teaching. In this way you form a connection with the Master, otherwise it is not possible to receive the Teachings or practise in a proper way. This is a preparation and is called Guru Yoga.

After that, read the Teachings of the Master and meditate in that way for twenty minutes. You should be clear that you have understood the Teaching before you begin to meditate, otherwise it is like trying to do business without having any capital! You must have some capital before you can set up a business and in the same way, you must understand this Natural State before you can meditate. If you feel drowsy or not very clear then hold your breath strongly and exhale strongly once – it can help you to wake up. If you have no problem then there is no need to do this. You can't stop or block disturbances or thoughts from arising, but when they appear, try to return to the Natural State as quickly as possible.

After each period of meditation, visualize that the Master comes down and integrates with you. There is no separation between you. This is how to integrate the Natural State with the rest of our life. It is very important to integrate as much as you can and stay in the Natural State. So do Guru Yoga at least once a day, or two or three times if you can. If you can get up a little earlier in the morning and do Guru Yoga early then it can be clearer.

The Nine Dersheg-Buddhas

Kuntu Zangpo

Thugjei Tonpa

Trulpai Tonpa

Rigpai Tonpa

Trulshen Nangden

Barnang Khujyug

Zangza Ringtsün

Chimey Tsugphü

Sangwa Düpa

The Masters

Lhabön Yongsu Dagpa

1. Lhabön Yongsu Dagpa

This Master was a Deva or Lha and was born in the realm of the Thirty-Three Gods on top of Mount Meru. He met the ninth Buddha of the Buddha Lineage, received this Teaching, practised and kept it carefully until he found his pupil, Lubön Banam, who was from the Naga-race. Lhabön Yongsu Dagpa taught his pupil everything but in particular he transmitted the Teaching of the Single Lineage:

"Mind is unborn. It is as boundless as the sky. Clouds and wind, light and darkness, these appear spontaneously in the sky but don't block space. So when you concentrate and remain in the Natural State, this Nature self-appears spontaneously. There is neither subject nor object. There is no need to practise meditation in a special way or focus on anything. This Nature is called Buddha Nature or Bön-Nature. There is no way to search for it or find it, no way to focus on it, so simply leave it as it is."

---

[114] Tib. lha.
[115] Tib. sum bcu rtsha gsum lha gnas.
[116] Tib. ri rab lhun po.
[117] Tib. bon nyid. Synonymous with Tib. chos nyid which is used in Tibetan Buddhist texts to translate Skt. dharmata.

Lubön Banam

2. Lubön Banam

Lubön Banam received the Teaching from his Deva-Master. He practised this Dzogchen Teaching of the Single Lineage and became a great Siddha.[118] He taught this Teaching to his human disciple.

"Our own Natural State is the Nature of Bön. This Natural State is not separate from our own Nature of Mind. Once you realize this Nature it neither shifts nor changes, neither increases nor decreases. Once this is realized by itself, that is Great Dharmakaya.[119] If you are not deluded but remain stable and free from disturbances, then that is excellent meditation."

---

[118] Tib. grub thob.
[119] Tib. bon sku.

Mibön Tride Zambu

3. Mibön Tride Zambu[120]

"The Natural State is the Nature of Bön. There is no special way to focus or meditate on it, neither is there any meditator nor anything special on which to meditate. There is nothing special which can be found, either as meditation or as meditator. Remain stable in the Natural State without any delusion. This is called 'No-Meditation' and 'Great Meditation'.[121] There is neither object nor subject; leave it as it is. That is the Great Meditation of the Dzogchen View."

---

[120] This Master was a native of Tagzig and was first in the human lineage.
[121] Tib. sgom med and Tib. sgom chen respectively.

Banam Kyolpo

4. Banam Kyolpo[122]

"The Natural State is the Nature of Bön and without focusing or meditating on anything particular you will achieve this state and find it out. If you don't focus or use your consciousness in any particular way, you will realize this Nature. The Nature knows neither ebb nor flow; it is always with you. If you believe[123] this Nature is the Natural State, then there is no particular way to meditate. Just leave it as it is."

---

[122] This Master was the first Zhang Zhung-pa in the human lineage. After him the lineage ran within Zhang Zhung until Pönchen Tsenpo who lived around 9th-10th century AD. He translated the Kagyud into Tibetan and gave it to Guge Loden who taught the *Nyamgyud* to Lhundrub Muthur and Shengyal Lhatse, thus the whole of the *Zhang Zhung Nyengyud* was transmitted within Tibet until Yongdzin Löpon Tenzin Namdak started teaching it in the West in 1989.

[123] Tib. yid ches. This is not normal belief or blind faith. In Dzogchen, this term refers to complete and firm trust based on the clear and stable realization of the Natural State of one's own mind.

Se Trisho Gyalwa

5. Se Trisho Gyalwa

"The Natural State has nothing to do with action. The more you fabricate, act or use your consciousness, the more thoughts you develop. This Nature has no meditation, it is completely empty Nature. Trying to focus, visualize or think merely makes a mess and you depart from the Nature. This Nature is focus-less, it is always in equanimity.[124] This is the real essential view of Tathagata[125] or Buddha."

---

[124] Tib. mnyam bzhag.
[125] Tib. bder gshegs.

Rasang Samdrub

6. Rasang Samdrub

"The Nature of Bodhichitta is Great Bliss.[126] It cannot be visualized as everything is absolutely as it is.[127] Simply keep in this state without delusion. This is called 'keeping on in the State without meditation'. This is the Great Meditation which is Great Perfection."

---

[126] Tib. bde ba chen po.
[127] A reference to transformative visualization techniques of Tantra which are not used in Dzogchen.

Darma Sherab

7. Darma Sherab

"When you have found the Nature of Mind, that is the root of the mind. When you have realized this Nature, maintain it without delusion. This is perfect Buddha-Mind or meditation, the Nature of Buddha. When you have found this state seek neither to alter nor monitor it; doing nothing to it, simply leave it as it is. This is Great Perfection. Since there is nothing which can be said to exist, there is no particular way to focus your mind or anything on which to meditate. Once you have realized this Nature, simply remain there."

Darma Bode

8. Darma Bode

Zhang Zhung Tripen asked his Master, "What is the meaning of the Nature of Mind?"

His Master replied:

"Look at a thought. There is neither colour, form nor anything material. It is like the sky. Yet this sky or space encompasses all that exists. This Nature cannot be fixed in words, neither can it be apprehended by consciousness; not even a Buddha can see it by means of consciousness. Without attempting to see through consciousness, the way to remain in the Nature is to simply leave it as it is without searching, finding or focusing on anything. Leave it as it is and that is excellent meditation. There is nothing to add; not even Buddha can change or add anything. Leave it as it is."

Zhang Zhung Tripen

9. Zhang Zhung Tripen

"Your own Natural State is perfected and integrated within Dzogpa Chenpo – Great Perfection or Great Bodhichitta.[128] This state which you have experienced is the great Dzogpa Chenpo; that is Dzogchen. No matter which name you give it – Great Perfection, Great Bodhichitta, or Buddha – everything is perfected in what you have experienced as the Natural State. No matter what you fabricate, no matter how much agitation or drowsiness arises, everything is within the Natural State.

The Natural State is called the Great Perfection of Bodhichitta. Without doing anything or searching for anything, simply leave this Bodhichitta or Great Perfection which you experience as it is. If you search or do something, you can't find anything. There is nothing special, nothing visible. This Nature has no root and there is nothing which can be found; it is very clear presence."

---

[128] Tib. byang chub sems.

Muye Lhagyung

10. Muye Lhagyung

"There are many words and many things to be said in the Teachings, but the essence is always the Nature. This Nature, called the Nature of Mind, neither grasps nor perceives anything. Seen from its perspective, the mind and consciousness are completely deluded. There is nothing particular to focus on within this Nature, nor is it possible to meditate upon it. If you focus on or think of it, you have lost your way, you are wrong. This Nature has neither subject nor object and is ever unborn. It is called Self-Born Wisdom.[129] Your meditation should be this: remain in equipoise in this Nature. This is real Bönku, the real knowledge of the Buddhas."

---

[129] Tib. rang byung ye shes.

Mashen Legzang

11. Mashen Legzang

"This Nature you have experienced doesn't depend on anything anywhere. There is no grasping, no perceiving, no binding thoughts. This Natural State is just kept as it is. That is the real meaning. You need only try to keep this Nature stable."

Gyershen Taglha

12. Gyershen Taglha

"It is important to release grasping and be introduced into the view of the Natural State. This view is free of the delusions of agitation, drowsiness and strengthlessness.[130] This is pure meditation. Once you have realized this Nature, your actions must be pure, in other words, untainted by the Five Poisonous Consciousnesses.[131] Whatever experiences you have while being in the Natural State, trust them."[132]

---

[130] Tib. rgod pa, bying ba, rmug pa. There are two types of agitation: rough and subtle. Rough agitation refers to the state when one is overwhelmed by a stream of strong thoughts which carry one away from the Natural State, blocking any progress in practice. Subtle agitation is the movements of subtle thoughts which gradually obscure meditation. These may go unnoticed for some time and even when they are noticed, one may not realize when and how they started. Drowsiness is the fault of becoming sleepy and sluggish resulting in a loss of presence. Strengthlessness is a lack of clarity in one's meditation. Meditation may still appear deep, calm and peaceful, but it does not progress; it is one-sided and can develop into mistaken fixation, mistaken Zhine (Tib. zhi gnas lding po), or even a meditative stupor (Tib. 'gog pa).

[131] Tib. dug lnga – five poisonous emotions: anger, jealousy, pride, ignorance and greed.

[132] This refers to meditative experiences (Tib. nyams) which arise during contemplation and enhance the practitioner's confidence (Tib. yid ches).

Rasang Yungdrungse

13. Rasang Yungdrungse

"Don't look at the past thought. Don't expect or look for the future thought. Don't grasp or perceive the present through consciousness."

The pupil asked, "What is the fault if you look for the past thought and what happens if you look for the future thought? What is the fault if you grasp the present with consciousness?"

The Master replied, "If you look for the first thought, you will not recognize the real Self-Wise Nature. If you expect the future thought, the flow of these thoughts will never stop. If you check for the present thought, you will never realize the illusion of developing visions and thoughts which arise one after another."

The pupil asked, "Then how can we practise?"

The Master replied, "Abide in Nature and do nothing; leave everything as it is."

Rasang Yungpen

14. Rasang Yungpen

"Don't look towards the past thought; whatever happens, just let it be. Don't grasp at the next thought. Cut off consciousness and thinking. All you need to do is remain like the sky."

Gepar Dondrub

15. Gepar Dondrub

"Keep in the equipoise of the Natural State without doubts. Keep in it without being deluded. Don't change anything either internally or externally. Don't concentrate on exhaling or inhaling. Don't use your consciousness and don't focus on anything. This is the method for practising."

Gyerpung Gepen

16. Gyerpung Gepen

"Keep the Bodhichitta of the Natural State naturally, loosely and comfortably. Don't keep any perceptions or grasp anything, leave everything open as it is. The illustration for this important Teaching is that it is like a man who has finished hard work."

Yongdzin Rinpoche adds:
This is only an example. Don't think that anybody is in the Natural State after they have worked hard, otherwise everyone could be a Dzogchen practitioner.

Se Gegyal

17. Se Gegyal

"Don't try to focus on any object with any part of your consciousness. Whenever spontaneous appearances arise within your consciousness, leave them freely and then your condition will be like the sun shining in the sky. Don't do anything. This Nature is clear, *salwa*, and aware by itself." [133]

---

[133] Tib. gsal ba. Rinpoche adds: "Here 'clear' means that space and the Nature are inseparable."

Zhang Zhung Namgyal

18. Zhang Zhung Namgyal

"How does one remain in the Natural State? Just leave it directly as it is. Don't remove any visions. If you leave whatever arises spontaneously just as it is, then it will become Great Wisdom. This teaching is a very important key for releasing all visions and matter and liberating them into the Nature."

Mugyung Karpo

19. Mugyung Karpo

"Once you have realized the Natural State, remain stable. As for all visions and movements of consciousness which appear spontaneously, just leave them alone while you yourself try to remain as stable as possible and become familiar with this Nature."

Horti Chenpo

20. Horti Chenpo

Horti Chenpo was a very important Master in those days because he held all the lineages of the Nine Ways[134] and was very learned in all of them. At first when his Master Mugyung Karpo began teaching him all the Nine Ways of Sutra, Tantra and Dzogchen, Horti Chenpo only wanted to learn Dzogchen, so he asked his Master for these Teachings alone. But his Master replied, "If you hold the Dzogchen lineage alone, what will you do if your pupils need another Teaching? You have to help all beings according to their capacity, so then what will you do? It may be enough for you personally to practise only Dzogchen but you must study and practise all these Ways because we never know what will be useful for other beings in the future."

Horti Chenpo's teaching:

"The view is impartial. The meditation is not focused yet clear. The activities are fully integrated with the Nature, they flow non-stop and unchecked. You don't need to expect the result, it will be received spontaneously. The view and result will appear spontaneously from the Nature. This is called the Activities of Dharmakaya."

---

[134] Tib. theg pa rim dgu.

Donkun Drubpa

21. Donkun Drubpa

"Leave all the actions of consciousness and all that consciousness receives and perceives just as is. Then, spontaneously, mental consciousness will be gradually released into Nature and this non-material Nature will become ever more blissful, Empty Nature. I think this is the view of the Buddha."

Rasang Pengyal

22. Rasang Pengyal

"Look into your consciousness. When you look towards the thought or consciousness, there is nothing special to see and you even lose the one who is looking and where he looks. This is the Great Nature. Everything liberates and disappears. There is nothing to do, nothing to change. Don't try to perceive anything. Leave everything as it is. Don't doubt, just keep on. This is the essential Teaching which is like Garuda flying in the sky."[135]

---

[135] This example of the great Garuda or Tib. khyung bird flying in the sky is often found in more elaborate Dzogchen Teachings. No matter what is beneath him, whether there are raging fires, ravines, precipices or storms, he does not care as nothing can affect him or sway his confidence.

Gurib Sega

23. Gurib Sega

"All the *thigles*[136] appear and everything is uncovered and clear. Nature has power and Wisdom emerges fully from the net of thoughts. Awareness comes into the State and this is the Nature of Mind."

Yongdzin Rinpoche adds:
Essentially, all the Masters teach in the same way to explain the Natural State which is spontaneously integrated with Trekchö and Thögal. In the Zhang Zhung Nyengyud the names 'trekchö' and 'thögal' are not used but the meaning comes together with the Clear Light.[137] The Teaching of Clear Light is that Trekchö and Thögal are practised together. Thögal is the capacity of this Nature, the essence of Nature, so when you have experience of the Natural State you have the essence of visions - many or few - because when you open your eyes some visions are always coming and going. That is the base of Thögal visions and as your practice develops, colours, shapes and so on appear. The Thögal visions develop as your practice develops; the two go together. This is sometimes explained with the example of water which always has the power or capacity to reflect; just as you cannot separate this capacity from water, so you cannot separate these visions from Nature. There is also a special method to develop practise Thögal visions using a little bit of body posture or gazes, but

---

[136] Tib. thig le – drop, sphere, bead, essence and so on. Here it refers to the drops or spheres of light which can be of one or more colours with a full *thigle* being a rainbow circle or sphere. A practitioner of Dzogchen begins to see full *thigles* in his/her contemplation when a certain level of stability in the Natural State is achieved. In later Dzogchen cycles, especially Buddhist ones, Dzogchen practice is divided into two stages: Trekchö, which corresponds with the empty aspect (Tib. stong) of the Natural State; and Thögal which corresponds with the clarity aspect (Tib. gsal); this line refers to the latter. Trekchö uses methods to stabilize one's realization of the Natural State while Thögal uses special methods which allow the practitioner to experience the energy of the Natural State manifesting through visions thereby leading him/her to the realization of the Rainbow Body of Light. In many Dzogchen cycles it is said that one must first become thoroughly established in the practice of Trekchö before moving onto Thögal. The *Zhang Zhung Nyengyud*, however, the most archaic Dzogchen tradition alive on this planet, does not use such a system and indeed does not use these terms.

[137] Tib. 'od gsal. Clear Light is the non-dual totality of the Natural State. This totality cannot be actually separated into clarity, emptiness and non-duality; these three terms are used to point to something which by its nature is inexplicable and beyond words. The *Zhang Zhung Nyengyud* has all the methods of Trekchö and Thögal but not the names. Since the Natural State has no divisions, there is no need to divide Dzogchen practice into two modes.

this is not practised separately. The important thing is that when you gaze into space and abide in the Natural State something is always moving, but all these movements of visions arise spontaneously from the Nature. You can't show them to another person, they are your own experience which spontaneously appears from Empty Nature. This is evidence that forms can appear in Empty Nature.

There are two ways to deal with this phenomenon: if you follow visions with your own consciousness they become more and more solid, like water becoming ice; ice is hard like a rock, and we think it is a real object, we don't think about water. It is the same when we always follow visions as objects; everything becomes sort of solid and that is our life. The other way to deal with this phenomenon is to go back to the source which is Empty Nature. That is Dzogchen. Once you go back to the source, don't try to jump out again. You need to trust and stay there. That is all.

24. Dawa Gyaltsen

Dawa Gyaltsen

24. Dawa Gyaltsen

Tsepung Dawa Gyaltsen taught Tapihritsa:

"Everything is vision so no matter what condition they find themselves in, the external universe and the beings within it are all integrated with the Natural State. That Natural State is called Basic Buddha. When visions appear they are without substance. They appear as Self-Awareness and without changing or being made, whatever appears simply abides in the Nature. This Self-Awareness cannot be separated from Empty Nature. There is nothing you can explain when you look back towards the Nature. This Nature is called the Spontaneously Abiding View of Buddha.

Whatever name you give things – 'sky', 'earth', 'rocks', 'pillars', 'father', 'mother', 'wars', 'vessels' – everything comes from this Nature. Whatever you call them, all phenomena are always equally integrated with the Natural State. If you check carefully you will discover everything which exists liberates by itself into the Nature and nothing whatsoever exists inherently.

Whatever we make – happiness, sadness, miseries – is created by consciousness and thought. Everything is created by thought and integrated with karmic cause. If you look at an object, you have it merely as a vision as there is nothing inherent which can be found on the object's side. That is called Empty Nature. If you examine the object, nothing can be found and what remains is the Nature. If you remain continuously in this Nature without changing anything, that is called the best meditation.

When you are stable in the Natural State, integrate all your everyday activities of body, speech and mind with this and they become Actions of Dharmakaya. The whole of existence is integrated and unified with the Natural State. Sometimes it is called Wisdom-Clarity, sometimes it is called thought, but both are equally integrated with Self-Awareness. Whether you create something through thought or whether you release everything into the Nature, everything is equally integrated with the Natural State. If on the other hand you follow thought or are just stuck in an indescribable sort of unconsciousness, Zhine,[138] without abiding in clarity then that is

---

[138] Tib. zhi gnas, Skt. Shamatha – Calm Abiding, the basic practice of calming one's mind applied within different levels of Yungdrung Bön, Buddhism and Hinduism. However, the application, function and understanding of Shamatha differ in the

called the Mistake of Shamatha. Even if you try to stop thoughts arising you cannot because the 'stopper' itself is also a thought. Thoughts arise incessantly and one thought cannot be stopped by another; it is better to leave them in Great Empty Nature. If you let thoughts rest in this Nature, then all consciousnesses and phenomena which exist will equally come to rest within it. Once you have experienced this Clear Nature there is no need to doubt it or try to grasp anything; it is better to simply leave it as it is and try to become familiar with it without fabricating anything. If you try to develop something using thoughts, if you wish to improve something or hasten your progress in meditation, then in fact although you expect and hope to find something, that is delusion. You cannot see the Nature with consciousness as whatever you do is an effort and thus disturbs this Nature. In fact, it cannot be disturbed by anything, but the practitioner is disturbed by these activities. Think carefully about what I have said and check it against your own experience.

There are four stages of development for those who practise Shamatha and each stage seems to be something similar to the Natural State, but in fact each one apprehends an object:

- The first stage of Shamatha is only concerned with infinite space.[139] It focuses on that side alone.
- The second stage of Shamatha is not to grasp or focus on the object itself but to look back to consciousness. Consciousness is unlimited so the focus becomes this unlimited consciousness.[140]
- The third stage of Shamatha is to examine both the object and the source of the consciousness which apprehends the object. You can't find anything on either side. There is nothing to find and nothing exists there. So the third stage is to focus on nothingness.[141]
- As for the fourth stage, it has already been established that nothing can be found, neither object nor subject, yet something indescribable exists, so this fourth stage is to focus on unspeakable nature.[142]

This is normal Shamatha and in each stage something is always

---

different traditions and even on various levels of the same tradition. The passage here refers to the mistake of 'being stuck' in emptiness, a blank state which has no clarity and is not the Natural State.

[139] Tib. nam mka' mtha' yas.
[140] Tib. rnam shes mtha' yas.
[141] Tib. ci yang med pa.
[142] Tib. 'du shes med min.

grasped as a point to focus on, therefore this cannot be compared with the Natural State.

As for the real Natural State, there is no focusing. There is neither object nor subject; just leave it as it is. That is the great Wisdom of the Unchangeable Swastika.[143] There is no dichotomy of object/subject, no focusing; the state is simply left as it is. It is called the View Without Teacher.

While you are abiding in the Natural State there is nothing which you can see as 'clarity' or 'empty nature'.[144] Don't focus or see or check or know anything, simply continue in contemplation. Without blocking anything, leave everything as it is in this State. It is called Self-Aware Wisdom.[145] Don't follow the monkey playing;[146] don't grasp or follow illusions like children playing in the sand.

This is the advice on how to maintain and practise the Natural State."

Yongdzin Rinpoche adds:
When you practise normal Shamatha there is always something to perceive, some focus. You can develop it so it becomes more stable, but it is incomparable with the Natural State. Why? When you practise the Natural State there is no perceiving or grasping as this state is completely beyond consciousness. Shamatha (and Vipassana[147]) on the other hand are always linked with consciousness. Shamatha can help calm your mind and develop various things, but you cannot compare it with the Natural State. It is very important for you to check the difference between perceiving and leaving everything open, just as it is, through your own experience. It is impossible to explain this distinction through the voice; you need your own experience.

---

[143] Tib. g.yung drung – the Bönpo swastika turning anti-clockwise which symbolizes the unchangeable Natural State.
[144] Tib. rang bzhin stong nyid.
[145] Tib. rang rig ye shes.
[146] i.e. don't follow the ordinary mind.
[147] Tib. lhag mthong – Insight Meditation.

Tapihritsa

25. Tapihritsa

Tapihritsa is especially important for us. Before him, twenty-four Masters transmitted the *Zhang Zhung Nyengyud* orally and nothing was written down; Sutra and Tantra were written down in Zhang Zhung at that time, but not Dzogchen. All the Masters had to learn the Teaching by heart and transmit it orally.

Tapihritsa received the Teachings from Dawa Gyaltsen and practised for nine years without any contact with other people in a place called Tagthab Sengei Drag[148] to the north-east of Mount Kailash. The place is still there and the name is the same although the population of the area has changed since then and most of the local people don't know about it nowadays. After practising for nine years Tapihritsa achieved Rainbow Body and disappeared. Before that he hadn't taught the Single Lineage of Dzogchen to anyone, but after achieving Rainbow Body he was ready to teach the Single Lineage to a pupil so he set about searching for a suitable, qualified student and he found one: Nangzher Lödpo. Nangzher Lödpo was head priest to the king of Zhang Zhung and an extremely proud man because he was not only very learned but also a powerful Tantric practitioner respected throughout the land. Although he had met with Dawa Gyaltsen and many other Masters, he was still not ready to practise Dzogchen. Nangzher Lödpo stayed in a cave on an island in Lake Darog[149] to the north-east of Mount Kailash. There are two lakes, one is salty[150] and the other, Lake Darog itself, is fresh water and he stayed there in a cave with some bushes around it. Nangzher Lödpo had a very rich donor[151] who often visited him, offering him food and anything else he needed. Finally both this donor and Nangzher Lödpo himself were ready to receive the Teachings so Tapihritsa emanated as a small boy and came to the rich man's doorway. This boy asked the rich man for food but he replied,

"You are a young man, why don't you work instead of begging?"

Tapihritsa said, "I can work but no-one has asked me to."

So the rich man answered, "Then stay here and work for me and I'll give you some money."

---

[148] Tib. sTag thabs seng ge'i brag.
[149] Tib. da rog mtsho.
[150] Called Tib. dra bye tshwa kha.
[151] Called Tib. sMer phyug po g.Yung drung rGyal mtshan.

Tapihritsa started to work for him, looking after his yaks and other animals, and he did everything very well. He was a good workman so the rich man called him 'Found Good Boy', Nyeleg.[152] One day Tapihritsa was out gathering firewood. He let the animals go off into the mountains and on his way back home he visited Nangzher Lödpo, who was meditating in the bushes near the cave. The boy came right up beside him but didn't prostrate or show any respect; he was just carrying wood. Nangzher Lödpo's pride was hurt because he was used to people being very respectful towards him but this boy didn't even prostrate to him. So he asked the stranger, "Why don't you prostrate to me?"

The boy said, "The sun or moon has no need to prostrate to or take refuge in an ordinary star. Big kings do not prostrate to small kings. No king salutes an ordinary person. Great Mahayana doesn't take refuge in Hinayana."[153]

When Tapihritsa offered those words to Nangzher Lödpo his pride was wounded even more and he wondered who the boy was.

"Who has educated you?" he asked. "Who is your Master? What are you carrying in your bag? And why are you working like this?"

Tapihritsa replied,
"My Teacher is all the visions of existence.
My load is thoughts.
I am working as a servant."

"If your Master is like ordinary beings and visions," Nangzher Lödpo remarked, "that means you have no Teacher. If you carry thoughts, that means you have no desire. If you are a servant, that means you have no happiness or miseries."

"If knowledge appears to you as experience," replied Tapihritsa, "then a Master cannot help at all. If you trust your experience, there is no desire which can disturb Nature. If everything arises as your own experience, there is no choice between happiness and misery."

When Tapihritsa said these words to Nangzher Lödpo he grew very angry:

"I see you are very educated and maybe you came to test me," he said. "Tomorrow morning I will go to see the king and I will call you for a debate in his royal presence. If you win, you will be my teacher. If I win, the king will punish you."

---

[152] Tib. khe'u rnyed leg.
[153] Tib. theg pa chen po and Tib. theg pa chung ngu respectively.

On hearing this Tapihritsa laughed for quite a long time. "Debate and logic are like playing and fighting," he said finally. "All discussions are like madness!"

Just then Nangzher Lödpo's donor came up and shouted at Tapihritsa:

"Hey, where are the animals? Why aren't you looking after them properly?"

Nangzher Lödpo realized that Tapihritsa was no ordinary boy but a very highly educated one, so when his donor shouted at him he was extremely shocked and both of them realized in a flash that they had committed a great sin. For a little while there were no more questions and neither of them had anything much to say. After some time the boy emanated a luminous light body in a rainbow circle and both Nangzher Lödpo and his donor saw it. Then the priest confessed his misdeed and offered all his gold to Tapihritsa saying,

"Take this, please. I confess, I criticized you harshly."

Tapihritsa said, "I am Tapihritsa. I came for you both. You are both ready to receive the Teaching. I don't want gold. I have no use for it, it is like offering it to a bird. Both of you listen to me carefully and I will give you the Teaching."

So they were ready to listen.

Taphiritsa's teachings:
"The Nature does not change and is not made. You cannot fabricate anything. This Nature simply abides spontaneously and you must try to experience it yourself. Self-Awareness[154] cannot be obscured. Self-Awareness has no thought, no thinking and no points for criticism. If you criticise it, then the criticism is of no use and is itself liberated "

Then Gyerpung realized how this true meaning applied to him and was deeply shocked; he suddenly fully understood the Nature.

That is Tapihritsa's teachings.

---

[154] Tib. rang rig.

Gyerpung Nangzher Lödpo

26. Gyerpung Nangzher Lödpo

Nangzher Lödpo became responsible for keeping the lineage and he asked Tapihritsa for permission to write it down, otherwise it could disappear, be destroyed or disturbed because Nangzher Lödpo lived in the eighth century during the reign of the Tibetan king Trisong Deutsen who invited Padmasambhava and other Indian Masters to Tibet, a time of terrible persecution for Bönpos. Trisong Deutsen murdered Ligmincha, King of Zhang Zhung, and Zhang Zhung was conquered by Tibetans; it was never independent again. Now this ancient kingdom is lost, completely integrated with Tibet. In these difficult times, Nangzher Lödpo made a pact with a very powerful Guardian,[155] the sky-god Nyipangse, subduing him and making him the special Guardian of the *Zhang Zhung Nyengyud*. Then Nangzher Lödpo was ready to teach the Single Lineage so he searched for a suitable student, but he could only find two people in the whole of Zhang Zhung. One was a seventy-three-year-old man called Gyalzig Sechung, the other, Mu Tsoge, was a three-year-old boy. Although Gyerpung had many students, few could receive the Single Lineage. The boy was too young, not yet ready to receive teachings, so he tried to teach the old man. In those days a Master had to select a student by asking the Guardians whether a person was suitable or not and by checking his manner in many ways. The old man was the King of Tibet's head priest,[156] a learned man who knew all the Nine Ways of Bön, especially Tantra, and he was ready to receive the Single Lineage.

"The Natural State has no substance; it is non-material. It is beyond thoughts, names and utterances. Don't try to give a name to this Nature. There is nothing certain to be recognized by consciousness. Neither focus nor meditate. Don't try to name it or say many things. This Nature is beyond examples, tales, stories, names and utterances. Don't search for examples, don't try to find anything particular as this Nature has no root and cannot be explained. Simply leave it as it is."

---

[155] Tib. bon skyong, srung ma.

[156] Tib. sku gshen. He appears to have been a Kushen of the king Ralpachan (Tib. Ral pa can), 815-836/866-901 AD who was Trisong Deutsen's grandson.

When Gyerpung said this to the old man he understood completely, practised continuously and was able to live one hundred and twenty years before taking Rainbow Body.[157]

---

[157] According to tradition, he lived 370 years.

27. Gyalzig Sechung

.

Gyalzig Sechung

27. Gyalzig Sechung

When the young boy Mu Tsoge turned nineteen, the old man was very old and gave him the Teaching:

"Buddha is unborn because it is not a result of causes produced by consciousness, words or actions. In the Natural State there is no reason to call anything 'buddha', no reason to call anything 'a being', because the Nature is empty, pure and without limits. Since this Nature knows neither the name 'buddha' nor 'being', it is unborn, non-stop and is integrated with all beings who have mind or consciousness. Wherever there is mind or consciousness, the Nature is there. As for the Natural State, there is no source from which it arises, nor is there anything visible where it abides at present. When one has experienced and realized this Nature, there is neither hope nor doubt; it is completely open, free and clear."

Mu Tsoge

28. Mu Tsoge

"You cannot call the Natural State either emptiness[158] or clarity. Even if you say it is a vision[159] or a view, there is nothing visible which can appear. If you say it is emptiness, there is no consciousness which thinks this. If you look into the Nature, you cannot even find Emptiness. If you think this Nature is permanent and unchangeable, there is nothing permanent to grasp or know. Even if you think it is nothingness, still you cannot see this nothingness. If you form a concept or try to show it, thinking: 'It is like this', you can neither conceive of nor demonstrate anything. If you say, 'It is a non-Nature, there is nothing to know, nothing to see, nothing exists' then that is nihilism, but there is no consciousness to hold this thought. The Nature is completely beyond thought or word. Just leave it as it is."

This practitioner lived a long time and finally this boy took Rainbow Body.[160]

---

[158] Tib. stong pa.
[159] Tib. snang ba.
[160] According to tradition, he lived 171 years.

Mu Tsotang

29. Mu Tsotang

This Master was born, received Teaching and practised in the Dangra area to the north-west of Central Tibet and his practice place[161] is still recognizable.

"The view does not have a particular way to look at itself. Therefore you must experience it and take the decision[162] to remain without hope and doubt. There is no way to focus on anything or grasp anything as meditation or non-meditation[163] as this State, the Nature, has nothing to do with consciousness. Therefore don't try to grasp anything or interfere using consciousness in any way. This Nature cannot be explained through the actions of body, speech and mind; there is nothing to say and nothing to do. Therefore you should release all the bindings of consciousness and thought – these are utterly artificial. Just leave your presence as clear as possible, leave it alone. This is the result of the view and practice. The Nature has nothing to do with speaking or thinking so you must cut through the binding of consciousness, thoughts, hope and doubt."

---

[161] Called Tib. shangs shel rong.
[162] Tib. yid ches. As already explained in footnote 123, this term refers to the obtainment of total confidence in one's realization of the Dzogchen view.
[163] I.e. Tib. sgom med.

Mu Shötram Chenpo

30. Mu Shötram Chenpo[164]

Mu Shötram Chenpo was a relative of his Master. Just below the glacier on Mount Targo[165] is a cave which was later called Shötram Phug,[166] Shotram's Cave, but nowadays people don't know why it is called Shötram and give the name a different interpretation. 'Sho tram' means 'playing dice'[167] so local people say the mountain gods play dice there!

"The Nature of Mind has no name. There is nothing which can be called 'this' or 'that', there is nothing which can be shown. As for what you have experienced as the Nature, don't doubt it, don't change or fabricate anything. Harbour neither hope nor doubt. Don't do anything. When the next thought comes, don't chase or change it, simply leave it alone. You shouldn't expect anything. Leave it as it is. That is the Nature".

---

[164] The iconography of this Master may seem a bit unusual in that he is depicted with fair hair. Bearing in mind that he was a native of Zhang Zhung it is perhaps not so surprising after all. Zhang Zhung comprised a confederation of 18 major tribes. The exact ethnicity of these tribes cannot be established with certainty at the moment. However, Zhang Zhung bordered Tokharian lands, who the Tibetans know as Thogar (Tib. tho gar), and it was here that some Bönpo family lineages, such as the Dru (Tib. bru) originated so it is not surprising that some of the Zhang Zhung population could have been of Indo-European descent. Tokharians or Yuezhi were fair-skinned, fair-haired people whose language was somewhat close to the Germanic family. For more on the possible interactions of Zhang Zhung/Tibetan Bönpo culture and Tokharians see Ermakov, *Bo and Bön*, pp. 8, 266, 272-273, 315, 713-714, 721, 726.

[165] Tib. gangs rta sgo.

[166] Tib. shod tram phug.

[167] Probably Tib. sho khram – 'cheat in dice'.

Mu Gyalwa Lodrö

31. Mu Gyalwa Lodrö

Mu Gyalwa Lodrö was a relative of his Master and until he was forty-seven years old he kept sheep below the Master's cave at Targo. One day, wolves killed some of his sheep. He was very sad, especially because some of the sheep had all their intestines taken out but were still alive. He didn't know what to do as he couldn't help much. If he left the sheep to get help, the wolves could come back and kill the rest.

He was fed up with his work and thought that his relative practising in the cave seemed to have an easier life. So he asked himself: why don't I do that, too? I have too many sufferings and miseries to put up with as a shepherd and my work is hopeless as wolves will always come. So the next day he stopped his work, went to see the Master and asked him:

"Is it possible for me to live as you do?"

"Yes, why not?" replied the Master.

So Gyalwa Lodrö gave up all activities and was always asking the Master to give him Teachings. Having finally received this Single Lineage, he practised continuously for the rest of his life. Then he in turn became a Master. He practised very intensively and realized Rainbow Body – it didn't take him long.

Mu Gyalwa Lodrö's teachings:

"Usually people talk about mind and consciousness, but if you look back to the source of the Nature of Mind, there is nothing particular which can be called 'mind' or 'consciousness' because there is no base whatsoever. When you find something which has no base and name it 'consciousness' that is your own creation.

With clear presence simply remain in the Nature without delusion. Whatever your experience, leave it as it is. No matter what feelings come up, don't care about them, follow or check them. Don't be deluded; in fact, there is nothing in this Nature which can be deluded. There is nothing particular or special underlying this Nature and there is nothing which can be put into words as there is no base at all."

His pupil Pönchen Tsenpo asked: "Why do you say 'don't be deluded'?"

The Master replied: "'Being deluded' is only a manner of speaking; if you look into the Nature, there is no place for delusion, no substance, nothing material, no base at all for either delusion or non-delusion."

The student asked: "If there is neither substance nor base, what then do you mean by 'delusion' and 'non-delusion' and 'nothing material'? What underlies the Natural State?"

The Master replied: "Well, after this, it is not possible to speak about it. Just remain present and clear in what you have experienced; keep it as it is. Whether your presence is clear or not, don't change anything, do anything or follow anything but simply leave it as it is. It is not important to check whether it is clear or empty and so on. There is no base at all. That is called the 'view of Dharmakaya'[168] which cannot be fabricated by any sentient being nor altered by even the Buddhas. If some Buddha or any being were to try to modify it, visualize it or express it, then everything would be artificial, it wouldn't be Nature. Were it to be created by someone, it would not lead to Buddhahood as everything would depend on something artificial or external which would not be the real, final truth. That would always lead to mistakes and delusion and, if one follows that, it doesn't lead to Buddhahood at all."

The student asked: "What is the view of Dharmakaya?"

The Master replied: "The view of Dharmakaya is that there is no base of Dharmakaya because there is no source whatsoever. What the 'clear presence'[169] means cannot be explained as there is no such place where the Nature abides in the present.

The student asked: "What is your practice, then?"

The Master replied: "I cannot explain what I practise, it is impossible to speak of it."

The student asked: "What do you do if thoughts come up?"

The Master replied: "Look at those thoughts. Where do they go? If you can't find the place they go to, then leave them. If you leave them, they don't go away from the Nature."

The student asked: "What is the result of this practice?"

The Master replied: "The result is that there is nothing particular to see."

The student asked: "What is Dharmakaya?"

The Master replied: "Dharmakaya is not material and there is nothing whatsoever which can be discovered. I can't even give you any example. The view of Buddha is such that it cannot be spoken of, nor shown, nor thought of, nor grasped. The Nature of Mind cannot be

---

[168] Tib. bon sku'i lta ba.
[169] Tib. rig gsal.

verified by consciousness at all because it has no base.[170] If there is no base, there is no need to search or study or try to grasp it. Don't follow thoughts as there is no thought-imprint which can be followed. Don't follow or try to stop any thoughts or visions, simply leave them alone freely. The Nature can be neither altered nor renewed. Don't hope or doubt. Don't try to practise or meditate or grasp or use your consciousness at all. Leave this Nature completely freely, open, without any grasping or attachment or application of consciousness. Release these completely. What is left behind is *hedewa*.[171] It is not possible to capture *hedewa* in words. *Hedewa* means something with no substance which cannot be grasped and at that moment there is not even any consciousness to think of it being empty or otherwise. What I am speaking about is nothing special, it is base-less. This Base of Nature[172] cannot be partitioned. No-one can give you an example, so just leave it as it is. Similarly, there is nothing which can be spoken of; you must just leave it as it is.

Sometimes we speak here about Buddha's view, but that is only words as, in fact, you can't find anything to call the 'view of Buddha' in Nature. If you practise this, there is nothing special to find and it is indescribable.

Then what should one do? Do nothing!

Then what is the result? The result is nothing.

Then what do you do? Don't rely on anything, it is clear by itself. This Nature doesn't depend on either Samsara or Nirvana, it exists by itself, and that is the Nature. Therefore we say it is beyond words or letters or thoughts. It cannot be shown through examples nor by using any method; it is simply not possible to show it to consciousness. This Nature is unborn and undying; these words [birth and death] hold no meaning for it. This Nature is unspeakable, unthinkable and is present very clearly – this is the view of Buddha.

---

[170] Tib. gzhi med.

[171] Tib. had de ba. Normally *hedewa* translates as 'startled mind' or 'totally blank state' and refers to the state of astonishment after being startled by something or the state devoid of thought after just having finished heavy work or woken up. As this state is utterly blank and without thoughts, it can be called 'empty'. However, it has nothing to do with the Natural State as it lacks Clarity and Awareness. Here *hedewa* is not used in this usual sense but refers to the inexplicable qualities of the Natural State.

[172] Tib. kun gzhi. This word, again, has widely differing meanings depending on the context. Sometimes it is synonymous with Tib. kun gzhi rnam par shes pa (Skt. Alaya Vijnana) or Basic Storing Consciousness, as Yongdzin Rinpoche often translates it, which stores all of an individual's karmic traces (Tib. bag chags). There are other meanings, too, but here it refers to the Natural State which is the Primordial Base of All.

This is the experience of the view of all the Buddhas which all the Masters practised successively and realized fully. The heart-essence of all the Teachings of the view of each successive Lineage Masters is collected here. This is the essence of Dzogchen which all the Masters practised and with which they achieved the final goal, and now it is shown to you."

After having been taught this, Pönchen Tsenpo visibly emanated as a cuckoo which flew away and disappeared into the sky, into the Dewa Chenpo.[173]

---

[173] Tib. bde ba chen po (Skt. Mahasukha) – Great Bliss. Here it refers to the full realization of the Natural State.

32. Pönchen Tsenpo

Pönchen Tsenpo

32. Pönchen Tsenpo

This is a very important Master. Tapihritsa had allowed the Teachings of the *Zhang Zhung Nyengyud* to be written down in the Zhang Zhung language and this Master translated them into Tibetan. He had several pupils and taught the Experiential Transmission lineage, the *Nyamgyud* lineage which we have here, but he also held the *Kagyud* lineage, which is the *Zhang Zhung Nyengyud* itself without the Experiential Transmission. He held these two lineages. The *Kagyud* lineage was taught to one pupil who came from faraway to the West, from near Ladakh.[174] Another pupil, from Tibet,[175] only received and held this Experiential Transmission lineage, so for several generations there were two different channels of transmission, then they came together again in a single Master.[176]

Pönchen Tsenpo had two principal Tibetan disciples to whom he taught the *Nyamgyud* lineage. The first was Pönchen Muthur and the other was Shengyal Lhatse. Before he met his Master, Pönchen Muthur was a very powerful Tantric practitioner but when he met his Master he was taught Dzogchen. From this Master only the Experiential Transmission was taught as the Single Lineage, not the *Kagyud Khorzhi*.[177]

Pönchen Tsenpo's Teachings:
"The Nature is without substance, therefore there is no Samsara. If you check all your visions, you can't find anything which exists inherently. Therefore there is nothing special which can be found as Nirvana. What, then, is the way to practise or meditate? Don't do anything in particular. If you check on your side – your consciousness, body etc. – there is nothing concrete which can be found. Therefore, there is nothing to do, no work to do."

Yongdzin Rinpoche adds:
When the Teaching says 'don't do anything' or 'nothing', don't think

---

[174] Tib. Gu ge Shes rab bLo ldan. See Introduction and the lineage diagram on page no.36.

[175] Tib. dPon chen Lhun grub Mu thur.

[176] See the lineage diagram on page no.36..

[177] Tib. bKa' brgyud skor bzhi – the four root texts of the *Zhang Zhung Nyengyud*.

that this is a kind of nihilism. The Teaching explains the real nature of Dzogchen itself, but we are Dzogchenpas, practitioners of Dzogchen, not Dzogchen itself. Dzogchen practitioners must take care and do practices such as Refuge and Bodhichitta as all the preliminary practices are needed. This Teaching may look like nihilism but it isn't. Nihilism means negating everything but in fact consciousness cannot grasp or negate or do anything else to Dzogchen itself. Dzogchen and Dzogchen-pa are different. A Dzogchenpa must take care to collect as many virtues as possible.

33. Pönchen Lhundrub Muthur

Pönchen Lhundrub Muthur

33. Pönchen Lhundrub Muthur[178]

Pönchen Muthur was a very great Tantric practitioner and most of the time he was occupied with Tantric practice. Even though he had received this Teaching, he was very interested in the power of Tantra and didn't concentrate properly on practising Dzogchen. He lived as a nomad with cattle, sheep, goats and so on. He had one white goat which looked after all the animals and a white female yak which looked after all the yaks so thanks to the power of his Tantric practice, there was no need to employ anyone. The animals looked after themselves.[179] That was how he lived, but at the end of his life he didn't disappear but left the body behind. Just before his death he

---

[178] This Master again is depicted with fair, almost blond hair. The reasons for that are similar to those already discussed in relation to Mu Shötram Chenpo. The difference is that this Master was actually Tibetan and we do not normally associate blond hair with modern Tibetans. However, there is an explanation justifying this iconography from the historical point of view. It is found in Christopher Beckwith's book *The Tibetan Empire in Central Asia: A History of the Struggle for Great Power among Tibetans, Turks, Arabs, and Chinese during the Early Middle Ages* (Princeton: Princeton University Press, 1987), p.6: "What may have been a crucial formative influence on the proto-Tibetans was migration of the peoples known in Chinese sources as the *Hsiao* (or "Little"-) Yüeh-chih, a branch of the *Ta* (or "Great"-) Yüeh-chih. After defeat by the Hsiung-nu in the second century B.C., the Ta-Yüeh-chih migrated to Bactria, and are generally identified with Tokharians, who according to Greek sources invaded and conquered Bactria at just that time. Those among them [or "Little" Yüeh-chich] who were unable to make the trip moved instead into the Nan Shan area, where they mixed with Ch'iang tribes and became like them in customs and language"; Ibid. p.7: "…Chinese sources recorded that certain Ch'iang tribesmen, after defeat by the Chinese, escaped deep into the Tibetan interior…" So this clearly shows that early Tibetans had an influx of mixed Ch'iang-Tokharian peoples. This is further backed by linguistic evidence: "The Tibetan verbal system is strongly reminiscent of Germanic tongues, but the language exhibits systematically entrenched proto-Indo-Iranian vocabulary. Together, these features indicate a relationship with the *divergent* "Indo-Tibetan" group, but the agglutinative grammatical structure, among other features (especially of modern spoken Tibetan), indicates a relationship with languages of the *convergent* Altaic group", Ibid. p.4, footnote 3. The proto-Indo-Iranian vocabulary is probably a result of much earlier influence coming with the Aryan migration and the initial spread of various types of Bön through Tibet-Qinghai Plateau. For references see footnote 164.

[179] He dedicated a white goat to Nyipangse and a white *dri* (Tib. 'dri) to Menmo Kumardza, the two principal Guardians of the *Zhang Zhung Nyengyud* and Zhang Zhung Meri Tantric cycle.

remembered how his Master had flown away as a cuckoo and realized that he himself hadn't practised Dzogchen properly but it was too late.[180] Nevertheless, he was a very powerful, renowned Tantric practitioner.

Yongdzin Rinpoche comments:
He practised Dzogchen once he had received the Experiential Teachings from Pön Tsenpo, but he didn't practise it seriously; he mainly practised Zhang Zhung Meri Tantra. Before he passed away, he said he was disappointed in three points:

- *He didn't concentrate on Dzogchen practice and that was a mistake for his practice.*
- *He was always proud of showing his powers which had come from practising Tantra. But that was not enough, so he was disappointed.*
- *He had wanted his life to be worthwhile and to be a great Dzogchen practitioner not a Tantrist, but he practised Tantra as well as Dzogchen and had great Tantric powers, so everyone knew him because of his power and came to him because of that. He was very proud and that had spoilt his life a little bit. He was very sorry for that.[181]*

He said honestly: 'I received very precious things but I didn't practise properly so now it is very late'. These three points were disappointments for him. [...] He said this very honestly. Modern lamas don't speak like this, but in those times he was very honest.[182]

---

[180] That is to say that he did not achieve Rainbow Body. Up to Lhundrub Muthur all Lineage-Masters of the *Zhang Zhung Nyengyud* achieved this realization. After him some Masters did whereas others didn't. However, even those Masters who did not realize Rainbow Body still attained an extremely advanced level of realization and so Yongdzin Rinpoche made this point while teaching *Nyams brgyud 'bring po sor bzhag*, the medium version of *Nyamgyud*: 'Don't think that he is just a Tantric practitioner, not a very good Dzogchen Master; he is good enough for us!' (Namdak, Yongdzin Lopön Tenzin Rinpoche. *Dringpo Sorzhag, Chapter II: The Clothes, Pith Instructions of Zhang Zhung Nyen Gyud Masters, Blanc, 15th – 17th September 2002,* Trnscr. & ed. Carol Ermakova and Dmitry Ermakov (Blou, Shenten Dargye Ling, 2006), Week 3, p. 65.)
[181] Extracted from: Ibid., Week 3, pp.60-61.
[182]Extracted from: Namdak, Yongdzin Lopön Tenzin Rinpoche. *Teachings on Zhang Zhung Nyen Gyud and Namkha Truldzö, Vimoutiers, 24 August – 11 September 2004,* Trnscr. & ed. Carol Ermakova and Dmitry Ermakov (Blou, Shenten Dargye Ling, 2006), Dringpo Sorzhag: Chapters VI – VII, pp. 53-54 (p. 44 Second Edition).

34. Shengyal Lhatse

Shengyal Lhatse

34. Shengyal Lhatse

Shengyal Lhatse was Tibetan, a contemporary of Lama Zurchen of the Nyingma tradition. They were good friends. When he was twelve or thirteen years old, his mother passed away and he had a very rough time because of his step-mother. He suffered for a long time and finally became very angry. He couldn't bear to live at home any longer so he ran away and went looking for magic to destroy his step-mother. As he wandered through Tibet, one day he saw some people playing dice and stopped to watch them. They gave him some food so he stayed there a while. They asked him where he was going but instead of replying he asked them if they knew of a powerful magician in that part of Tibet. It was in the west of Central Tibet. The dice players told him about Pön Lhundrub Muthur, who had become very powerful and famous. The boy decided to go and see him but when the people heard of his plan they warned him to be careful because the Master had several extremely fierce dogs that could eat him up. Undaunted, Shengyal Lhatse went to the Master's place, following the directions he had been given by the dice players who had advised him to go down to the river and wait for the Master's wife to come and collect water. He went to the river and sure enough after a while the Master's wife came to get water there, so they met. She asked him many questions about where he was going and what he wanted but he said he had heard that the Master was a very powerful Lama.

'Yes,' replied the Master's wife.

'How can I see him?' he asked.

'Can you work?'

'Yes, I can,' said Shengyal Lhatse and promised to help her.

So she took him home to work for her. When he came to her house the Master was not there, only his wife and some workers. The boy worked hard for several days without seeing Lhundrub Muthur, so finally he asked where the powerful Master was. 'Oh, he quite often goes to the mountains to meet his Master. He'll be back soon', said his wife. The boy continued to work very hard. After a while the Master came down from the mountains and asked the boy what he wanted. He explained that he wanted to destroy his step-mother. The Master taught him some Tantric practices and he still continued to work very hard. When the Master went back to the mountains again, his own Master, Pönchen Tsenpo, asked him:

'Do you have a boy who wants to learn black magic?'

'Yes, that is true, a boy has come.'

'He is a suitable student for Dzogchen. Bring him to me,' said Pönchen Tsenpo.

So the next time Lhundrub Muthur wanted to go to the mountains again he told the boy that the Lama had said to fetch him, so they both went to see Pönchen Tsenpo who always moved from one place to another in the mountains. When the Master Pön Tsenpo met the boy, he asked him what he wanted. The boy replied that he was searching for some very powerful magic with which to destroy his step-mother. Pönchen Tsenpo said:

'Oh, it's very easy to destroy her, not at all difficult.'

And he started to teach the boy how to practise Dzogchen. The boy worked very hard, learning and practising, and finally he found the view of Dzogchen Nature.

His Teacher asked him:

'Now what does your step-mother look like?'

'Oh, I have lost my step-mother!' replied the boy. 'There is no need to destroy her.'

'I destroy my enemies like this,'[183] said his Teacher.

The boy didn't reply, he just practised Dzogchen continuously and didn't care about his step-mother any more.

Pönchen Tsenpo taught Shengyal Lhatse:

"The Natural State has no foundation, no root or source. Don't give it any names. There is no need to recognize anything as existing externally so don't follow visions at all. Don't try to partition this Nature as it has neither side nor segments. The view of Dharmakaya has no partiality, no vision, no names and it is not possible to establish a direction – this side, that side, my side, your side – there are no sides. This is the view of all the Buddhas. This view of Buddha-Nature cannot be improved by Buddha, nor can even the cleverest beings change it. It is impossible to point out anything material or visible in it; that is the view of the Buddhas. This is the only Nature and nothing can show or describe it to you. This state is simply called Empty Nature. Don't grasp it by consciousness as consciousness cannot know it, therefore don't give it any names."

Lama Shengyal Lhatse spontaneously realized the meaning through his experience and he could neither alter nor show what he had experienced. He explained this to his Master and the Master said,

---

[183] I.e. through realizing the view of Dzogchen any concepts such as 'enemy' and 'friend' are naturally 'destroyed' as they dissolve into their source.

"That is called the Wisdom of Self-Awareness.[184] No-one can practise better than this and no matter how much you practise, the Nature doesn't improve with practice, it simply becomes more stable for you. If you practise more, this state will always be the same, it will merely remain stable for longer. This Nature never grows better or worse, so there is no work for *sem*[185] or consciousness. There is nothing special to see and consciousness liberates into Nature. Soon even this consciousness gradually disappears. The Natural State simply appears temporarily, spontaneously, but if you follow these manifestations, you find no substance and no result.[186] Therefore there is no need to do anything or use material things; everything is Empty Form.[187]

This Nature knows neither birth nor death. Death or birth, it doesn't matter as the Nature will always be the same. This Natural State can be neither altered nor developed. Therefore, this Basic Nature shows nothing and that is the Great View of Dzogchen. Just remain in this view for as long as possible and try to stabilise it. That is meditation. Try to make what you practise stable. That is the only fruit; don't expect anything. Sometimes thoughts can appear spontaneously but don't try to follow them and they will disappear without trace. If thoughts arise spontaneously there is no need to doubt or be frightened – they don't make any trouble. The state knows neither my side nor other's side, neither friend nor enemy, so don't follow or check anything. No matter what thoughts come up, leave them alone and they will disappear without trace. Once they disappear, there is no need to check where they have gone or whether any trace is left. There is no need to verify or think. There is no dualism[188] of object/subject. Awareness[189] has no support, it is only naked, clear presence; that is the Nature of Buddha."

He received this from his Master and the idea of his enemy step-mother liberated completely and became a friend.[190]

---

[184] Tib. rang rig ye shes.

[185] Tib. sems.

[186] This refers to the aspect of clarity which manifests as visions indicating one's progress in the practice of Clear Light. However, these visions have no material substance and dissolve back into the Kunzhi, the Base of All, so there is no material result which can be grasped or used in any way.

[187] Tib. stong gzugs.

[188] Tib. gnyis med.

[189] Tib. rig pa.

[190] Since there is nothing which can disturb someone who has thoroughly realized the Dzogchen view it is said that all appearances, thoughts and emotions, be they negative

Once Shengyal Lhatse had received the Teaching he was always practising in the mountains moving from place to place. One day a nomad[191] was looking after sheep on the Targo range near Lake Dangra when he met a man with no shoes carrying only a bag with nothing but a skull cup inside it. His clothes were very poor. Very surprised that the man was roaming the mountains barefoot, the nomad asked him,

'Where are you from?'

'There is no certain place where I come from.'

'Where are you going? Where are you staying?'

'I have no place to go and no place to stay.'

The nomad was very surprised and thought the man was probably a wonderful yogi-practitioner,[192] so he offered him his food but the man hardly took anything. Then the nomad offered him his shoes, saying,

'You have no shoes, you'd better have mine.'

'No,' replied the strange man. 'It is better if you keep your own shoes. If I put your shoes on my feet, what shall I do when they wear out? You keep your shoes.'

So then the nomad said, 'I have a house. Come to my home.'

'No, that's impossible. I'm just like a wild animal, it's not possible for me to come down to the village or somewhere else.'

This nomad had heard about the boy who had run away from home and gone in search of magic to destroy his step-mother and thinking he had found him, he caught the man, carried him home and kept him in his temple. In fact, the nomad was a rich man so he said to his captive,

'You stay here and I will feed you and give you all you need.'

'But I am a sick man,'[193] said the yogi, 'and you'll probably get sick, too. Let me go.'

'No, no!' replied the nomad. 'We want to keep you in my temple. You practise there, I don't want to let you out.'

So he fed him and let him practise in the temple. Meanwhile, there was a village meeting. The rich nomad went along and told the villagers that he had caught Pönchen Tsenpo's pupil in the mountains, the boy who had escaped from home to look for magic. 'It is marvellous that I've found him,' he said. 'I'll keep him and never let him out.'

or positive, are like a friend as they all point to the Natural State.

[191] He was one of three Kyibar (Tib. skyid 'bar) brothers who became Shengyal Lhatse's sponsors.

[192] Tib. rnal 'byor pa.

[193] He bluffed by saying that he had leprosy.

So the nomad helped Shengyal Lhatse build a hermitage, and indeed, it is still there now in the Dangra area. Although it was destroyed, it has now been rebuilt as a small monastery and goes by its original name Yungdrung Lhatse after the hermit who practised in the cave.[194] This Master Shengyal Lhatse was a contemporary of Zurchen, a Nyingmapa. They were friends.[195]

Shengyal Lhatse's pupil was Lhagom Karpo. He was very learned. He was about to complete his final religious education and needed to get some offerings for the ceremony,[196] so he was carrying molasses with him on his horse to sell and exchange for butter, to celebrate his degree. On his way he stopped for the night somewhere, and while he was there he overheard people talking about a practitioner who lived in a nearby cave. As soon as he heard about him, Lhagom Karpo was overwhelmed by very strong devotion and broke into tears. He resolved to go and see that Master. In the morning the people he was staying with woke him very early because they had to make a journey. When he asked them where they were going, they said they were planning to visit a very special yogi who lived in a cave not far from there. When he told them he wanted to go with them, they warned him, saying,

'OK, but the Master might not accept you.'

'He has to,' replied Lhagom Karpo. 'My devotion is very strong.'

So he loaded his bag onto his horse and they set off.
On seeing the yogi, he was filled with devotion and requested some initiation or other. The Master said that he should have a special initiation, so he put his hands on Lhagom's head for a while.

'Has your head grown hot from my hands?' asked the Master.

'Yes,' confirmed his student. That was the initiation.

Lhagom stayed there with the Master and offered him his own horse. Shengyal Lhatse asked his assistant to bring the horse. 'Your master gave you to me and now you have to stay here,' he said into the animal's ear. The horse never went far away.

---

[194] The monastery Tib. g.yung drung lha rtse'i dgon pa was built around the cave where he practised and rebuilt at the request of Yongdzin Rinpoche.

[195] See Introduction.

[196] A degree similar to what is now known as Geshe degree (Tib. dge shes kyi go gnas), or Doctor of Religion (Philosophy). The ceremony involves a very elaborate, lavish ritual.

Shengyal Lhatse taught Lhagom Karpo:

"If you look into the object, into all visions and visible things, you can't find anything which exists inherently or concretely so there is absolutely nothing to meditate upon or practise. If you realize that there is nothing whatsoever which exists inherently, then you don't need to hope or doubt anything; simply continue to abide clearly in the Nature.

There is no root, no base, no object, nothing that can be caught by consciousness. There is nowhere this Nature can stay, you cannot point to where it is, there is nothing you can recognize, nothing. There is neither hope of attaining some result nor disappointment if you don't see or know something. There is just clear presence.

I have understood the Nature like that. If you understand what I said and keep on practising, maybe you will have the experience," he said. "I think that is important."

35. Lomting Lhagom Karpo

Lomting Lhagom Karpo

35. Lomting Lhagom Karpo

"There are six faults:
As for the view, it is unstable, like a bird's feather which is always blown by the wind.

Activities which you try to integrate with the Nature will always disturb you at first. If you meditate, it disturbs your work. If you work, it disturbs your meditation, so you are like a bird with a broken wing.

When you meditate, no experiences arise; there is nothing special to see, just as when you watch the sky.

When you enter the path or start to practise, there is nothing special to say or do, so you are like a blind man left in the middle of a meadow.

Whatever you say, your words have no connection to the real meaning, so you are like a parrot speaking.

Whatever you think, nothing has any particular result, so you are like a poor lady who makes all sorts of plans, but nothing is realized.

These are six examples. Don't let your meditation be like this."

His pupil Ngödrub Gyaltsen Ringmo asked,
"If I don't follow the errors of these six examples, what shall I do then?"

The Master replied:
"Keep the view as the sky with no end, no centre and no side. It is itself clear.

As for activities,[197] act without support and whatever you do, always try to integrate everything with the practice of the Nature.

Your wisdom is always clear without partiality. Whatever you do, always try to integrate everything with the Nature. That is the meaning.

The way to enter into practice and realize this Nature is by looking at your own body or that of another person; when you examine it you can't find anything inherent. Yet you must still integrate with the Ten Virtues[198] without neglecting or abandoning

---

[197] Tib. spyod pa.
[198] Tib. dge ba bcu. These are: protecting and saving life; giving and not taking what is not given; not engaging in sexual misconduct; speaking truthfully; not gossiping

them. If you realize and practise all Ten Virtues integrating them with meditation, then you have found a Great Method. Without being influenced by speech or thought, don't follow or trust anything but try to integrate with the Nature. That is essential. Always try to abide in this Nature and practise with it, and then you will gradually come to realize Clear Self-Wisdom.[199]

When you recognize the Natural State clearly, then your practice, meditation and experiences come together. If you do this and practise more and more, meditative experiences will come and you will certainly find this Nature yourself and be satisfied and happy.

That is how you will find stable meditation. That is the meaning of not following these six examples. Try to remember and practise these six points."

Again the Master said to him,

"As for the view, meditation and activities,[200] don't try to focus on or grasp anything, simply try to integrate with Nature and practise. If you do not focus on or grasp at anything or at nothingness, then that is meditation. The example is like the ocean: remain with neither desire, nor grasping, nor thoughts – that is the view. If you desire the eternal, that is your own desire; don't follow it.

If you look towards the Nature, there is nothing special to do, nothing to follow or stop. Leave everything spontaneously as it is. That is the precious golden sun shining. When you are familiar with this Nature, there will be no desire or wish to receive anything. That is meeting Dharmakaya. That means you have purified the fire of thought. If you purify the fire, then there is no smoke of desire. Thus the sun of the Clear Light[201] shines brightly and the darkness of the Alaya[202] will disappear. You will experience the non-stop meditation and become familiar with it. Thus you will be released from rebirth, death, old age and sickness. Moreover the seeds of delusion and thoughts will be ultimately purified. Then you will no longer return to Samsara and will find stable devotion within the Nature."

---

but reciting mantras and prayers; speaking gently; speaking words which bring accord and harmony; rejoicing in others' accomplishments; keeping loving thoughts towards all; having the right view regarding the Teachings and worldly affairs.

[199] Tib. rang rig rang gsal.

[200] Tib. lta ba, sgom pa, spyod pa, bras bu – view, meditation/practice, conduct/activities, fruit/result.

[201] Tib. 'od gsal.

[202] Tib. kun gzhi rnam shes.

The current lineage holder:
Yongdzin Lopön Tenzin Namdak

Yongdzin Lopön Tenzin Namdak Rinpoche

Tenzin Namdak was born into a nomad family in Khyungpo,[203] Khamnyi,[204] in East Tibet in 1926. His early childhood was not easy and at the age of seven he went to the nearby Tengchen monastery[205] where he learnt to read and write. His uncle, Tsering Yang Phel, and his maternal grandfather were renowned artists and when Tenzin Namdak was around thirteen or fourteen he went to Yungdrung Ling monastery[206] with his uncle to paint murals in the new temple there. The work completed, Tenzin Namdak refused to leave, staying on to take full ordination instead.

It was when he was a teenager that he first met his Teacher, Sanggye Tenzin. They met on several occasions in several places, including Lake Namtso[207] where the young Tenzin Namdak had been accepted as a disciple by Gangru Rinpoche,[208] the former Lopön of Yungdrung Ling monastery. He spent four years practising and studying with Gangru Rinpoche in a cave there. During this time, Tenzin Namdak learned the *Atri* Dzogchen cycle as well as the sciences and arts[209] such as astrology, medicine, poetry, grammar, composition, and the proportions and consecration rituals for *chörten*,[210] statues and *mandalas*. Due to lack of paper, he traced his letters in the ground and learned everything by heart.

However, it was not until Sanggye Tenzin was appointed Lopön of Menri monastery that Tenzin Namdak began to study with him intensely, at the age of twenty-four. A few years later, when he was around twenty-seven or twenty-eight, he began receiving the main teachings of the *Zhang Zhung Nyengyud* and continued studying with his Master until the latter passed away in early 1978.

In 1957 Tenzin Namdak passed his Geshe degree with flying colours at Menri and was immediately made Lopön there. He retired in 1957 to devote himself to personal retreat at Dangra Lake, a region where some of the early Dzogchen Masters of the *Zhang Zhung Nyengyud* Dzogchen had practised. Learning of the Chinese invasion,

---

[203] Tib. Khyung po.
[204] Tib. Khams nyi.
[205] Tib. sTeng chen dgom pa.
[206] Tib. g.Yung drung gling dgom pa.
[207] Tib. gnam mtsho.
[208] Tib. sGang ru Rin po che.
[209] Tib. rigs gnas.
[210] Tib. mchod rten (lit. support for offerings/worship), Skt. stupa (lit. heap) – a monument symbolizing the Buddha's mind with a complex external form and internal structure filled with many relics and holy objects. In Yungdrung Bön there are 360 types of *chörten*: 120 which can be constructed physically, 120 which can be visualized and 120 *chörten* of Empty Nature.

he tried to flee his homeland in 1960, but was shot and wounded by a female Chinese soldier. After about ten months in a Chinese prison, Lopön Tenzin Namdak managed to escape, eventually finding his way to Nepal. As a result of all the upheaval and suffering of the Chinese Communist takeover, Tenzin Namdak lost touch with his Master Lopön Sanggye Tenzin and could only presume he, like so many other Tibetans, had perished.

In 1961 Tenzin Namdak was befriended by Prof. Snellgrove who invited him to England where the young Lopön worked at SOAS, the University of London, as well as learning English in Cambridge where he met Chogyam Trungpa and Akong Tulku. During this time Tenzin Namdak travelled widely in the UK and did a retreat in a Benedictine monastery on the Isle of Wight. He also supervised the building of a Bönpo stupa, Yungdrung Koleg Chörten[211] the height of a man in Prof. Snellgrove's private garden. In 1964 he heard that his Teacher was alive and well in India, so Tenzin Namdak went to join him.

At this point he found himself in charge of a displaced and destitute band of exiled Bönpos, many of whom were monks who died or fell ill as they worked on the roads in the unfamiliar heat of India. Lopön Tenzin Namdak set about rescuing and preserving his Yungdrung Bön tradition by shouldering the responsibility of finding land for a Bönpo settlement, and by salvaging and publishing many Bönpo texts. Having arranged accommodation for his Master, he himself sheltered in a garage for several years, somehow successfully publishing precious texts through the American Library of Congress, New Delhi.

In 1967, Lopön Tenzin Namdak finally managed to secure funding for a piece of land as well as houses for each Bönpo family, at Dolanji, Himachal Pradesh, thanks to a generous grant from the Catholic Relief Service. However, he now faced a new challenge: he personally designed the houses for all seventy Bönpo households, even down to calculating the number of bricks needed. The settlement flourished, with a monastic centre being established under the guidance of Lopön Sanggye Tenzin and Lopön Tenzin Namdak in the 1970's, despite a lack of teaching texts. At this stage, the two Lopöns concentrated on teaching the *Zhang Zhung Nyengyud*. By 1986 a full cannon of teaching texts had been printed and the first Geshes graduated.

In 1978, Namkhai Norbu Rinpoche visited Dolanji together with a small group of Western students, where he received teachings

---

[211] Tib. g.yung drung bkod legs mchod rten.

on the *Zhang Zhung Nyengyud* and subsequently invited Lopön Tenzin Namdak to teach in Merigar, Italy and other Dzogchen Community centres in Europe and the USA.

Lopön Tenzin Namdak established a second monastic centre, Triten Norbutse, in Kathmandu, Nepal, in 1987 which has been recognized by H. H. the 14th Dalai Lama as an exemplary monastic institution. Monks and nuns still make the perilous journey over the Himalayas to study there under this most erudite master.

In 1991 Lopön Tenzin Namdak was first invited by H. H. the 14th Dalai Lama to represent the Yungdrung Bön tradition at a Kalachakra initiation, in New York.

Lopön Tenzin Namdak has been giving Dzogchen teachings in the West since 1989 to a growing group of committed students. In 2005 a centre, known as Shenten Dargye Ling, was established in France and Lopön Rinpoche spends several months there each summer giving Dzogchen teachings and instructing his Western students on other aspects of the Yungdrung Bön tradition.

Yongdzin Lopön Tenzin Namdak Rinpoche's teachings:
It is very important to integrate your daily life with the practice of the Natural State as much as you can. Whenever you remember the Nature, it is there; it never goes away.
My advice is to try to concentrate with the Natural State every day. That will help you in this lifetime and in the next, until you reach Buddhahood.

Final remarks

The purpose of what I have been teaching here is to show you how to practise on a daily basis for the rest of your life; it is not just something limited to these few days here. We have learnt how to do Guru Yoga and to abide in the Natural State. What is the purpose of remaining in the Natural State? When you abide in the Natural State, depending on how stable and familiar with it you are, your obscurations, defilements and emotions can be purified. That is real essential religion and practice.

Thögal visions are not explained in detail here but hopefully as we meditate everyone opens their eyes and remains in the Natural State as stably as possible and when you gaze into space, you are bound to see some movements in front of your eyeball. These movements aren't created by yourself but exist spontaneously whether you have realized Nature or not. All beings have them, but they don't know what they are. This is the beginning of Thögal. The visions are already there so as you practise and become familiar with the Nature, they appear spontaneously. As you practise more, these visions become clearer and take shape, just as butter forms if you churn milk. If you get excited and expect to see something, visions don't come, but if you don't expect or reject anything, then they appear by themselves. So that is the real purpose, that is the Nature.

Dzogchen doesn't apply visualization techniques; there is neither expectation nor doing because everything is the Nature. If we find this Nature, then visions are proof of its power:[212] they are evidence of how our life manifests from Empty Nature. But if we follow after these visions they become ever more solid, like water turning into ice. Indeed, we have been 'practising' this solidification for a long time. There is a single source but two ways of 'practising' or behaving and this second one, following visions, leads to Samsara. If, however, you look back to the source instead of following the visions, then that leads to Nirvana. Once you realize how to practise correctly, even though it looks like just sitting back and resting, it has a great purpose. We are humans who can understand what we are doing and what awaits us in the future, not just some years ahead, but in the next life and further lives. If we practise, our condition will be more useful and fruitful. We are training for that now. When you realize that all life – the external universe and the internal sentient

---

[212] Tib. thugs rje.

beings 'self'[213] – comes from Empty Nature and is nothing but Empty Form, there is no need to follow attachment to external phenomena. As you practise and realize Empty Nature, gradually your clinging will become weaker and weaker. It is important to check the Natural State by yourself; this has been said many times. It is important to try to make it clear to yourself. This is the real foundation. If it is not so clear, you can still meditate and practise, but we cannot be sure how useful that will be.

There are eight main consciousnesses[214] plus many branches, fifty-one altogether. Each of them acts by grasping or catching different objects. The Natural State is not consciousness. You have to experience this by yourself. You can understand this clearly when you create a thought and look at it: where is it? Just after you look back towards it, it disappears. There is nothing to be found, just an unspeakable state. How long this state lasts depends on your practice. This state is pure Nature, not a consciousness. You have to realize this state, and this method shows it clearly. However, if even after this you carry on watching on any level that means you still haven't found the Nature which is beyond consciousness. When you look back towards a thought, there is a completely open state without grasping: stay there. You have to have this experience.

Presence is what exists in the present, and this Awareness is the opposite of unconsciousness. It is also beyond any consciousness, pure or impure. In deep sleep there is no awareness. If you look to where thought disappears and keep what is there just as it is without modification, that state is not like deep sleep as there is clarity and presence; that is Awareness. This Awareness or clarity is not consciousness; it is empty and self-clear. You have to trust that state. If you don't trust but keep looking or changing it, then you will never find the Natural State. All kinds of consciousnesses are connected with thought or mind but when you abide in the Nature, clarity is there. Clarity is empty and self-clear, just as a lamp which is lit is clear by itself and needs no other light. Clarity and emptiness are inseparable, non-dual.

When you are in deep sleep, consciousness is liberated into the Alaya or Store Consciousness, but it is not in the Natural State at that time. When you practise and have the experience of the Natural State, then thoughts or consciousness, as well as all kinds of visions, are spontaneously liberated into the Nature: your presence is clear and

---

[213] Tib. bdag.
[214] Tib. rnam shes brgyad.

you are in the Nature. The difference is that while you are in the Natural State your awareness is clear but when you are in deep sleep you have no awareness, it simply looks like unconsciousness. Every being has a different mind or consciousness – if one person is angry, not everyone is angry. Where there is mind, there is the Nature just as where there is water, it is wet. When applied to the Natural State, the term 'non-dual' doesn't mean that all consciousnesses are inseparable. Rather, it means that the Natural State's qualities of emptiness, clarity and spontaneous appearances are inseparable. So wherever there is the Nature there will always be emptiness, clarity and unification.[215] If you look back to your thought, the first thought disappears and the next thought has not begun yet there is a state which you cannot fully describe. This state has clarity, emptiness and unification; they are all there, but it is not possible to separate emptiness, clarity and so on, you have to have experience.

As you learn more and more you will have clear proof of your progress. As you practise more and more you will become familiar with this real Nature. The more familiar you are with it, the weaker all other visions will become. That is why you need to practise more. If you practise with visions, for example in a dark room,[216] you still see lights, colours and forms even though all external light is blocked. This isn't just lies or stories from a long time ago; you can experience it for yourself. These lights come from the Nature and are evidence that our whole living condition is an illusion. All the visions are our own vision and they increasingly integrate with our visions of everyday life until finally they become one. Practitioners who see their own everyday visions as illusions can go through rocks and mountains and that in turn is proof that nothing exists inherently. Such a practitioner isn't showing some magic, just the truth about the real state of everything. We can talk about this but it is not easy to have real trust without having your own experience. So you have been shown the map, now you have to practise.

A word on practising in modern times

Sometimes I read you the biographies of the Lineage Masters who spent their whole life in a cave. So maybe some of you think of cutting off your living conditions and going and living like that. But that is not

---

[215] Here Yongdzin Rinpoche uses 'unification' for Tib. nyis med – 'non-dual'.
[216] This refers to the practice of dark retreat or Tib. mun mtshams.

possible in modern times.[217]

It is important to understand this. According to the times we live in, usually, don't think that you should go away from some certain place to search for solitude or something. You can read history or biographies of the early Masters, but that time is over. You have to think: we are now in modern society. It is not easy. In early times, especially in Tibet – although not all Tibetans were practitioners, not at all – some people would first study and gain knowledge, and then realize, and then practise. They would spend their whole life in solitude. In those days, if someone went into solitude seriously then anybody nearby who saw them staying in some cave somewhere would immediately serve them and help them. The local people knew that the practitioner was a living person who needed simple things like firewood, food, tsampa or some simple things. They would serve the practitioner willingly. He would not be living in luxury at all, but he would not be starving, so in that way he could spend his time practising continuously. Those practitioners were real, living people but they didn't care about their worldly conditions. I mean, they didn't expect or prepare any living conditions at all because they already knew someone would help them, in those days. But that time is over. The texts are still there, the system is still the same, it is written here, but if you do this nowadays, you will starve if you don't prepare anything, you see. Follow the teachings but don't follow what these Masters did. If you try to, you will be starving or freezing!

In modern times it is better for practitioners to prepare. I am always talking about our two conditions. Whatever you are doing in your lifetime to ensure your living conditions, you should carry on with that, but don't have too high expectations or go after a reputation; that doesn't help very much. But you have to do something to earn a living. Otherwise, we call it Ngejung[218] *– you collect many different teachings, you listen to many different Masters and suddenly you think: 'Oh, this life is no use!', and you stop everything and try to concentrate on practice for a little while. But your property, possessions and facilities won't last so long. If you go back and try to carry on with your job, relationships and so on afterwards it is really hard to find work. So it is better to carry on continuously in a simple way, not doing anything special, not having too high expectations, not expecting luxury, but just living in a simple way.*

Then alongside that it is very important to try and think about

---

[217] Extracted from: Ibid. *Namkha Truldzö*, p. 101 (Second Edition p.143).
[218] Tib. nges 'byung – renunciation.

preparing for the next stage; death will certainly come, there is no doubt. You have to do some preparation by yourself; no-one else can do anything. We can see that. Just after someone has passed away their house or bed is cleaned up and then the next morning other people move in. Nothing remains and soon no-one can remember you. No-one will be able to help you at that time; maybe they will be able to say some nice things and put you in the coffin in a comfortable way, but that doesn't help at all. Think about it, there is just the skeleton lying in the coffin, nothing else, so whether it is comfortable or not doesn't help. The mind went away a long time ago, and no-one can be certain where it is roaming now – higher realms, lower realms, circulating who knows where. What is the situation at that time? Don't think this next stage is an illusion or not true or something. It feels just as it does now in this present time. You can see evidence of this in dreams; they show you. Dreams are great evidence. So try to trust what dreams show you as this is evidence for what it will be like when you leave your body.[219]

As for how to prepare for this next stage, I hope you can read again and again what I was saying earlier. That is preparation, that is what to do.[220]

---

[219] When we dream, whatever experiences we have seem just as real and tangible as our waking life; this is the same after death, when the mind wakes up in the intermediate state between death and the next life (Tib. bar do).

[220] Extracted from: Nyachen Lishu Tagring, *Yangtse Longchen*, Teachings by Yongdzin Lopön Tenzin Namdak Rinpoche, trnscr. & ed. Carol Ermakova and Dmitry Ermakov, Shenten Dargye Ling, France, 27 July – 15 August 2008, pp. 236-237.